P9-DEG-726

THE
PRESSURE OVEN
COOKBOOK

BY MARIAN GETZ

Copyright © 2015 Marian Getz
All rights reserved. No portion of this book may be reproduced, stored in a retrieval system, or transmitted in any form by any means, mechanical, electronic, photocopying, recording or otherwise, without written permission from the publisher.

Printed in the U.S.A.

TABLE OF CONTENTS

Your pressure oven is going to make cooking easier and faster than using a regular oven. Foods are juicier and crispier from cooking with pressure. You will wonder how you ever lived without one. Here are a few tips to help you get started.

The pressure oven combines the cooking methods of a pressure cooker and an oven. In order to cook with pressure, a few extra steps are required to what you might be used to from a regular oven. Below are some tips to help you get the most out of your pressure oven.

Setting the Timer:
Please note than in order for the cooking process to start regardless if you're using pressure, the Timer Knob needs to be set. If you wish to use a separate kitchen timer you can do so but remember to set the Timer Knob of your oven to start the cooking process.

Cooking Modes:
Your pressure cooker can be operated with or without pressure. Most recipes in the book require cooking with pressure. Simply follow the steps in the recipe and review your manual for further operating instructions.

Baking Rack Positions:
Please note the particular baking rack position in each recipe and follow directions. Generally, tall foods require the rack to be in the lower position. If your oven has a rotisserie you will not be able to fit the roasting pan in the center position so it needs to be placed in the lower position. Generally, broiling is done with the baking rack in the upper position to get the food as close to the heating element as possible.

Additional Cooking Time:
Some recipes require a second cooking cycle after the first one. In those cases, use the original method of cooking (pressure or no pressure) then reset the oven to the original temperature and function settings (unless otherwise stated) and set the timer according to the additional cooking time needed per the recipe instructions.

Cooking Times exceeding 2 Hours:
The oven's timer has a 2 hour limit for safety reasons. Some recipes in this book require cooking times exceeding 2 hours such as pot roast and brisket. In order to cook longer, let timer expire after 2 hours or turn the timer off then turn it back on to the desired remaining time needed to complete the recipe.

Monitoring Food:
If you want to monitor your food or check for doneness, release the pressure according to the instruction manual, open the door then check your food and restore pressure to continue cooking. The steam is restored instantly when you seal the door again so you are not delaying the cooking by opening the door.

Avoiding Messy Cooking:
For foods that tend to drip like pies, pizza or casseroles, place a pan or aluminum foil under them to avoid a big mess. I prefer HEAVY DUTY aluminum foil in the 18-inch long box as the size fits universally in most pans and holds up well.

Preventing Over-Darkening:
Foods cook fast in this oven and can darken quickly. A piece of aluminum foil can significantly reduce over-darkening, especially foods that are tall like turkey. Pinch foil around areas like the ends of drumsticks or lay a piece of aluminum foil loosely over larger pieces such as chicken breast.

Covering Food with Foil:
Many recipes call for foods to be tightly covered with foil and 4 slits to be cut into the foil. This is done to allow the food to retain moisture and not dry out. In addition the slits are necessary to allow the oven to utilize the moisture to create steam for the pressure cooking.

Special Food Comments:
Foods that contain eggs or a significant amount of liquid have a tendency to puff up when you turn the vent release valve and raise the sealing lever. Also, liquids will boil up rapidly which is normal and should be expected due to the use of pressure.

You can cook turkey breasts in this oven however because the average turkey breast at the store comes from a 20+ pound turkey, it will take significantly longer to cook than a whole turkey (Turkey in Under 1 Hour recipe on page 6) as it is a big, dense piece of meat).

For large cuts of meat or poultry, let stand at room temperature for 1 to 1 1/2 hours before cooking. The meat will become juicier and cook more evenly. Just let it sit out while preparing other parts of the meal.

Using Nonstick Cooking Spray:
When using the Drip/Baking Pan with Broil Rack Insert for fish or delicate foods, please apply nonstick cooking spray to the rack so that your food does not tear into pieces when you remove it.

Seasoning:
The recipes in this book are written by a chef so they are written to be delicious. This means they will be well seasoned, contain fat and possibly sugar. If you like to use less sodium, fat or sugar, please do so in the manner you usually do. Also I make use of bouillon bases that are sold in jars as a paste. They are much easier to keep and use than boxes of stock or the dry cubes. The boxes of stock are mostly water, are weak in flavor and are difficult to carry home from the store. Bouillon bases come in many flavors including vegetable and they add a tremendous flavor to your meals.

Leftovers:
You will notice there are many recipes that call for leftover turkey and chicken. Now that you have an oven that will make you delicious, juicy chicken and turkey you will want to make them often so having a repertoire of recipes that use up leftovers is a smart way to cook. All of the recipes that call for leftover turkey or chicken will be delicious with either form of poultry so use whatever you have on hand.

Cleaning the Oven:
When the oven is cold and unplugged, use a soft scrub sponge and just wipe away. The sponge slides easily under the heating element and is therefore the best way to clean the oven.

Meat Thermometer:
Many recipes call for the use of a meat thermometer to check for doneness. Undercooked meat can pose a health concern and overcooked meat can ruin a meal. The proper method of using a meat thermometer is to insert it into the thickest part of the meat without touching the bone. Test in more than one area for best results. For thinner, flat pieces of meat such as steaks, chops and chicken breasts, insert the thermometer horizontally to get the most accurate reading. Please refer to the cooking chart included in your pressure oven manual for recommended temperatures or follow USDA's recommendation.

Trussing Poultry:

Trussing involves tying your poultry with kitchen twine so that the wings and legs are fastened against the body. This allows your poultry to cook more evenly, keep its shape and fit better into your oven. You will need about 2 feet of kitchen twine and scissors. Please follow the below steps for proper trussing:

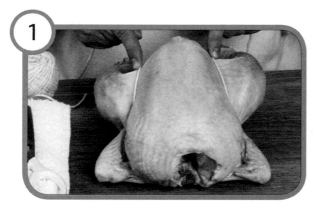

Place the poultry on a cutting board breast up. Place twine under the wings then pull the twine evenly between legs and breast.

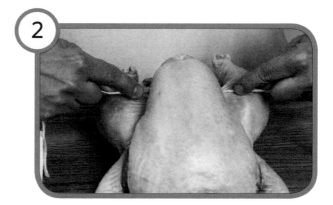

Cross the twine.

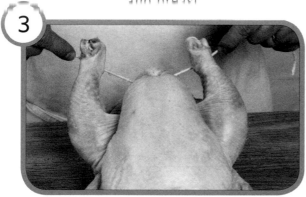

Run the twine under the end of the legs.

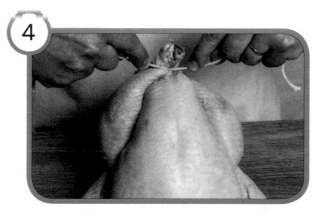

Wrap the twine up and around legs, bring them together then tie the twine into a knot and a bow to secure.

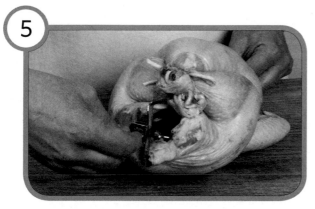

If using the rotisserie, run rotisserie rod through the cavity of the poultry. Secure the rotisserie tine between the legs and into the back of the poultry then tighten down the screw on the rotisserie tine.

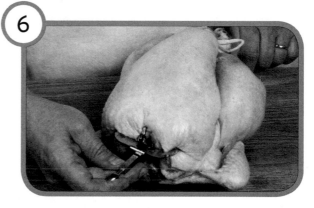

Place the other rotisserie tine on the rotisserie rod already inserted. Slide down and secure the rotisserie tine into both sides of the breast. Tighten down the screw on the rotisserie rod. Load into the oven.

Turkey in Under 1 Hour

MAKES 8 SERVINGS

1 turkey (10 pounds), thawed
1 tablespoon olive oil
Kosher salt and fresh pepper to taste

1. Remove turkey from refrigerator. If desired, for a crispier skin and more even cooking, let the turkey rest at room temperature for 1 to 1 1/2 hours. Otherwise proceed to next step.

2. Rinse the turkey under cold water then remove neck from cavity and giblets from neck cavity.

3. Pat turkey dry using paper towels. Place the turkey in the roasting pan, follow the trussing instructions on page 5 then drizzle with oil and season with salt and pepper.

4. Preheat the oven to 450°F, set the function to ROAST and timer to 10 minutes.

5. Place the pan on the rack in the lower position then close the door.

6. Set the Vent Release Valve to SEAL, lower the Sealing Lever to the SEAL position and reset the timer.

7. Roast turkey for 50-55 minutes or until well browned and juices are boiling.

8. When cooking is complete, turn the Vent Release Valve to VENT and wait for all air to escape. Once vented, slowly raise the Sealing Lever and press the Door Release Button to open the door.

9. Internal temperature of turkey should register 165°F on a meat thermometer. If necessary, repeat step 6 and roast for an additional 5-10 minutes until 165°F internal temperature is reached.

10. Allow turkey to rest for 15 minutes before carving.

11. Use flavorful juices in roasting pan to make gravy, if desired.

This turkey cooks in a short time and does not usually develop the typical dark color. In order to achieve a darker color, mix 2 tablespoons of soy sauce and 1 tablespoon honey until the honey dissolves then brush mixture all over turkey skin before roasting.

Apple Butter Pulled Pork

MAKES 4 SERVINGS

1 jar (18 ounces) apple butter
1 cup apple juice
2 tablespoons jarred chicken bouillon base or to taste
Kosher salt and fresh pepper to taste
3 pounds pork shoulder

1. In the roasting pan, whisk together all ingredients except pork.

2. Place the pork in the pan, turn over to coat the top with some of the mixture, cover tightly with aluminum foil then cut 4 small slits into the foil for steaming purposes.

3. Place the pan on the rack in the lower position then close the door.

4. Set the Vent Release Valve to SEAL, lower the Sealing Lever to the SEAL position and set the timer.

5. Set the oven to 325°F and function to ROAST.

6. Cook for 3 hours or until meat is fall-apart tender.

7. When cooking is complete, turn the Vent Release Valve to VENT and wait for all air to escape. Once vented, slowly raise the Sealing Lever and press the Door Release Button to open the door.

8. Remove the pan, skim excess fat from juices, pull pork into chunks using tongs then serve as desired.

Apple Crumble

MAKES 4 SERVINGS

FOR THE APPLES:
1/2 cup unsalted butter, melted
1/2 cup light brown sugar, packed
1/4 teaspoon kosher salt
1 teaspoon ground cinnamon
4 tart apples, sliced

FOR THE STREUSEL:
1 cup oatmeal
1/2 cup all purpose flour
1/4 cup light brown sugar, packed
1/4 teaspoon kosher salt
1/4 teaspoon baking powder
1/2 cup unsalted butter, softened

1. Preheat the oven to 450°F, set the function to BAKE and timer to 10 minutes.

2. In the roasting pan, stir together the butter, brown sugar, kosher salt and cinnamon.

3. Place the pan on the rack in the lower position then close the door.

4. Set the Vent Release Valve to SEAL, lower the Sealing Lever to the SEAL position and reset the timer.

5. Cook for 3 minutes or until fragrant and sugar begins to brown.

6. When cooking is complete, turn the Vent Release Valve to VENT and wait for all air to escape. Once vented, slowly raise the Sealing Lever and press the Door Release Button to open the door.

7. Immediately add the apples and stir to coat with the caramel in the pan. Some caramel will harden as it touches the apples.

8. Repeat step 4 then cook for an additional 5 minutes.

9. While apples are cooking, stir together all streusel ingredients in a bowl. Use your fingertips to pinch the butter into the oat mixture until clumpy but no visible dry flour remains.

10. After 5 minutes, remove apples then pour streusel over the top.

11. Repeat step 4, lower temperature to 350°F and cook for an additional 15-20 minutes or until brown and bubbly.

12. Remove and serve as desired.

BBQ Chicken Pizza

MAKES 2 SERVINGS

1 store-bought pizza dough ball (8 ounces)
All purpose flour, for the dough
2 tablespoons bottled BBQ sauce
1 1/2 cups mozzarella cheese, shredded
2 tablespoons Parmesan cheese, grated
1 cup leftover chicken or turkey, diced
2 tablespoons red onions, sliced
Kosher salt and fresh pepper to taste
Fresh cilantro, for serving

1. Preheat the oven to 450°F, set the function to BAKE and timer to 10 minutes.

2. Stretch the dough into a rough rectangle or desired shape using flour to prevent sticking then place in the roasting pan or on a pizza screen.

3. Brush or spoon the BBQ sauce over the dough then top with both cheeses.

4. Scatter the chicken and onions over the top then season with salt and pepper.

5. Place the pan on the rack in the middle position then close the door.

6. Set the Vent Release Valve to SEAL, lower the Sealing Lever to the SEAL position and reset the timer.

7. Bake for 7-10 minutes or until well browned and bubbly (turn pizza around halfway through cooking if desired).

8. When cooking is complete, turn the Vent Release Valve to VENT and wait for all air to escape. Once vented, slowly raise the Sealing Lever and press the Door Release Button to open the door.

9. Remove pizza, garnish as desired, top with cilantro and serve.

TIP

Add some condiments you already have in your refrigerator to any pizza such as capers, pepperoncini peppers, olives or sun-dried tomatoes.

TIP

Add 2 pounds of small potatoes to the pan and place the meat on top before roasting. The meat juices and fat will give the potatoes a delicious taste.

Prime Rib

MAKES 8-10 SERVINGS

1 boneless prime rib or rib roast (6 pounds), tied
1 tablespoon olive oil
2 tablespoons kosher salt
2 tablespoons freshly cracked pepper
1 tablespoon garlic, chopped

1. Rub roast with oil then place in the roasting pan.

2. In a small bowl, mix together remaining ingredients then rub all over the meat and let stand at room temperature for 1 hour.

3. Place the pan on the rack in the lower position then close the door.

4. Set the Vent Release Valve to SEAL, lower the Sealing Lever to the SEAL position and set the timer.

5. Set the oven to 450°F, function to ROAST.

6. Cook for 120 minutes for rare or 115°F on a meat thermometer. Add about 10 minutes cooking time for medium-rare, 20 minutes for medium and 30 minutes for well done. Adjust if necessary until desired doneness is achieved.

7. When cooking is complete, turn the Vent Release Valve to VENT and wait for all air to escape. Once vented, slowly raise the Sealing Lever and press the Door Release Button to open the door.

8. Remove meat, let rest for 15 minutes then carve into desired slices and garnish as desired before serving.

Best Pulled Pork

MAKES 6-8 SERVINGS

3-4 pounds boneless pork shoulder
Kosher salt and fresh pepper to taste
2 cups pork or chicken stock
Bottled BBQ sauce of your choice, for serving

1. Place pork in the roasting pan, season with salt and pepper then pour over the stock.

2. Cover tightly with aluminum foil then cut 4 small slits into the foil for steaming purposes.

3. Place the pan on the rack in the lower position then close the door.

4. Set the Vent Release Valve to SEAL, lower the Sealing Lever to the SEAL position and set the timer.

5. Set the oven to 450°F and function to ROAST.

6. Cook for 3 hours or until meat is fall-apart tender.

7. When cooking is complete, turn the Vent Release Valve to VENT and wait for all air to escape. Once vented, slowly raise the Sealing Lever and press the Door Release Button to open the door.

8. Remove pork, skim off excess fat using a spoon then use tongs to shred or pull-apart the pork.

9. Garnish as desired and serve with BBQ sauce.

TIP

Do not use mild flavored Cheddar cheese or the taste will be bland.

One Pan Mac & Cheese

MAKES 4-6 SERVINGS

3 cups dry elbow pasta
4 cups water
2 tablespoons jarred chicken bouillon base or to taste
2 teaspoons dry mustard powder
1/2 cup whole milk
8 ounces shredded sharp Cheddar cheese

1. Line the bottom and sides of the roasting pan with heavy duty aluminum foil.
2. Combine the pasta, water, bouillon base and mustard powder in the pan and stir gently.
3. Cover tightly with aluminum foil then cut 4 small slits into the foil for steaming purposes.
4. Place the pan on the rack in the lower position then close the door.
5. Set the Vent Release Valve to SEAL, lower the Sealing Lever to the SEAL position and set the timer.
6. Set the oven to 450°F and function to BAKE.
7. Cook for 35 minutes.
8. When cooking is complete, turn the Vent Release Valve to VENT and wait for all air to escape. Once vented, slowly raise the Sealing Lever and press the Door Release Button to open the door.
9. Remove pan, discard the top sheet of foil then add remaining ingredients and stir using a wooden spoon until all the cheese has melted (return the pan to the oven and cook on BROIL for 6-7 minutes to brown the top if desired).
10. Remove pan, garnish as desired and serve.

┌─────────── TIP ───────────┐

For a nice, brown chicken, brush
with a mixture of 1 tablespoon
soy sauce and 1 teaspoon honey
before seasoning with salt and
pepper.

└────────────────────────────┘

Simple Rotisserie (or not) Chicken

MAKES 4 SERVINGS

1 chicken (4 pounds)
Kosher salt and fresh pepper to taste
1 tablespoon olive or canola oil

1. Drizzle oil on chicken then liberally season with salt and pepper.

2. If using the rotisserie, place chicken on rotisserie rod and use the lifter to place in the oven. Otherwise, place chicken in the roasting pan and tie snuggly following trussing instructions on page 5.

3. If not using the rotisserie, place the pan on the rack in the lower position then close the door.

4. Set the Vent Release Valve to SEAL, lower the Sealing Lever to the SEAL position and set the timer.

5. If using the rotisserie, set oven to 450°F and function to ROTISSERIE. Otherwise set oven to 450°F and function to ROAST.

6. Cook for 35 minutes or until internal temperature reaches 165°F on a meat thermometer.

7. When cooking is complete, turn the Vent Release Valve to VENT and wait for all air to escape. Once vented, slowly raise the Sealing Lever and press the Door Release Button to open the door.

8. Remove chicken from rotisserie using the lifter tool or remove the pan.

9. Let rest for 10 minutes before carving then garnish as desired and serve.

Blueberry Cobbler

MAKES 6 SERVINGS

For the Blueberries:
6 cups fresh or frozen blueberries
3 tablespoons unsalted butter, melted
2 tablespoons all purpose flour or cornstarch
1/2 cup granulated sugar or other sweetener
1 tablespoon lemon juice
1/4 teaspoon kosher salt
1/4 teaspoon ground cinnamon

For the Streusel:
1 1/4 cups all purpose flour
1/4 cup granulated sugar
Zest from 1 lemon
1/4 teaspoon kosher salt
1/4 teaspoon baking powder
1/2 cup unsalted butter, softened

1. Combine the ingredients for the blueberries in the roasting pan and stir well.

2. Combine all streusel ingredients in a large bowl. Use fingertips to pinch the butter into the flour mixture until clumpy but no visible dry flour remains then pour streusel evenly over the blueberries in the roasting pan.

3. Place the pan on the rack in the lower position then close the door.

4. Set the Vent Release Valve to SEAL, lower the Sealing Lever to the SEAL position and set the timer.

5. Set the oven to 325°F and function to BAKE.

6. Bake for 30 minutes or until streusel is well browned and blueberries are bubbly.

7. When cooking is complete, turn the Vent Release Valve to VENT and wait for all air to escape. Once vented, slowly raise the Sealing Lever and press the Door Release Button to open the door.

8. Remove cobbler, garnish as desired and serve.

Fall Apart Pork Chops

MAKES 4 SERVINGS

Kosher salt and fresh pepper to taste
2 large yellow onions, sliced
2 garlic cloves, minced
1/4 teaspoon dried sage

1 can (10.75 ounces) cream of celery soup
1/3 cup whole milk
1 cup chicken stock
4 large pork chops

1. In the roasting pan combine all ingredients, except pork chops. Stir until most of the soup is smooth then add pork chops and turn to coat.

2. Cover tightly with aluminum foil then cut 4 small slits into the foil for steaming purposes.

3. Place the pan on the rack in the lower position then close the door.

4. Set the Vent Release Valve to SEAL, lower the Sealing Lever to the SEAL position and set the timer.

5. Set the oven to 375°F and function to BAKE.

6. Cook for 70 minutes.

7. When cooking is complete, turn the Vent Release Valve to VENT and wait for all air to escape. Once vented, slowly raise the Sealing Lever and press the Door Release Button to open the door.

8. Remove pan, discard foil, garnish as desired and serve.

My Favorite Glazed Ham

MAKES 6-8 SERVINGS

1 boneless carving-style smoked ham (4-5 pounds)
1/4 cup water
1 cup ketchup
1/3 cup yellow mustard
1 1/3 cups light brown sugar, packed

1. Place ham in the roasting pan then pour 1/4 cup water around the ham.

2. In a bowl, whisk together remaining ingredients until smooth then pour half over the ham evenly, reserving the remainder for serving.

3. Place the pan on the rack in the lower position then close the door.

4. Set the Vent Release Valve to SEAL, lower the Sealing Lever to the SEAL position and set the timer.

5. Set the oven to 325°F and function to BAKE.

6. Cook for 60 minutes or until deeply caramelized and internal temperature reaches 140°F on a meat thermometer.

7. When cooking is complete, turn the Vent Release Valve to VENT and wait for all air to escape. Once vented, slowly raise the Sealing Lever and press the Door Release Button to open the door.

8. Remove ham, garnish as desired and serve.

19

Rosy Roast Beef

MAKES 4-6 SERVINGS

4 pounds eye-of-round beef roast, tied
1 tablespoon jarred beef bouillon base or to taste
Kosher salt and fresh pepper to taste
2 Russet potatoes, chunked

2 carrots, cut lengthwise
1 large yellow onion, chunked
1 tablespoon canola oil
A few sprigs fresh thyme

1. Preheat the oven to 450°F, set the function to ROAST and timer to 10 minutes.

2. Using gloves, rub meat all over with the bouillon base, salt and pepper.

3. Pour the potatoes, carrots and onions into the roasting pan, drizzle with oil then season with salt and pepper.

4. Place beef on top of the pan contents then top with thyme.

5. Place the pan on the rack in the lower position then close the door.

6. Set the Vent Release Valve to SEAL, lower the Sealing Lever to the SEAL position and reset the timer.

7. Cook for 45 minutes or until well browned and desired temperature is reached (115°F for rare, 125°F for medium and 135°F for well-done on a meat thermometer).

8. When cooking is complete, turn the Vent Release Valve to VENT and wait for all air to escape. Once vented, slowly raise the Sealing Lever and press the Door Release Button to open the door.

9. Remove and let rest for 10 minutes before serving with the vegetables and pan juices.

Steamed Pesto Salmon

MAKES 4 SERVINGS

4 salmon fillets (6 ounces each)
Kosher salt and fresh pepper to taste
4 tablespoons jarred pesto + more for serving

4 fresh lemon slices
4 sprigs fresh thyme or rosemary
1/2 cup white wine

1. Fit the broil rack insert into the drip/baking pan then apply nonstick cooking spray to both.

2. Place salmon fillets on the broil rack, season with salt and pepper then spoon some pesto over each fillet.

3. Add lemon, herbs and wine around the salmon.

4. Place the pan on the rack in the middle position then close the door.

5. Set the Vent Release Valve to SEAL, lower the Sealing Lever to the SEAL position and set the timer.

6. Set the oven to 450°F and function to BAKE.

7. Cook for 7-10 minutes or until salmon is mostly opaque and flakes easily.

8. When cooking is complete, turn the Vent Release Valve to VENT and wait for all air to escape. Once vented, slowly raise the Sealing Lever and press the Door Release Button to open the door.

9. Remove salmon, garnish as desired and serve with additional pesto.

Cheeseburger Pizza

MAKES 2 SERVINGS

1 store-bought pizza dough ball (8 ounces)
1 tablespoon ketchup
2 teaspoons yellow mustard
4 ounces ground beef, cooked and crumbled

1 tablespoon yellow onions, chopped
4 American cheese slices
7 dill pickle slices
Kosher salt and pepper to taste

1. Preheat the oven to 450°F, set the function to BAKE and timer to 10 minutes.

2. In the roasting pan, stretch pizza dough into a rough rectangle or desired shape. Stir together ketchup and mustard then spread onto dough and top with remaining ingredients.

3. Place the pan on the rack in the middle position then close the door.

4. Set the Vent Release Valve to SEAL, lower the Sealing Lever to the SEAL position and reset the timer.

5. Cook 7-10 minutes or until well browned and bubbly.

6. When cooking is complete, turn the Vent Release Valve to VENT and wait for all air to escape. Once vented, slowly raise the Sealing Lever and press the Door Release Button to open the door.

7. Remove pizza, garnish as desired, cut into slices and serve.

Brown Sugar Pork Tenderloin

MAKES 4-6 SERVINGS

1 large yellow onion, sliced
1 cup pork or chicken stock
2 pork tenderloins (about 2 pounds total)
1 tablespoon olive oil
Kosher salt and fresh pepper to taste

2 tablespoons brown mustard
1 tablespoon bottled soy sauce
1/3 cup light brown sugar, packed
2 teaspoons onion powder

1. Place onions and stock in the roasting pan then place pork on top. Season with oil, salt and pepper.

2. Place the pan on the rack in the lower position then close the door.

3. Set the Vent Release Valve to SEAL, lower the Sealing Lever to the SEAL position and set the timer.

4. Set the oven to 450°F and function to ROAST.

5. Cook for 15 minutes then turn the Vent Release Valve to VENT and wait for all air to escape. Once vented, slowly raise the Sealing Lever and press the Door Release Button to open the door.

6. Remove the pork and set aside.

7. In a small bowl, combine remaining ingredients then bush mixture over the pork.

8. Repeat step 3 then cook pork for an additional 10 minutes or until well browned and internal temperature of pork registers 155°F on a meat thermometer.

9. Remove from oven, let rest for 5 minutes then slice and garnishing as desired before serving.

Lazy Sunday Pot Roast

MAKES 4-6 SERVINGS

2 tablespoons soy sauce
1 beef chuck roast (3-4 pounds)
2 tablespoons olive oil, divided
Kosher salt and fresh pepper to taste
2 bay leaves

6 small potatoes
1 medium yellow onion, chunked
1 carrot, chunked
1 celery stalk, chunked
2 cups beef stock

1. Brush soy sauce all over the roast then season with salt and pepper. Drizzle with half of the oil.

2. Place remaining ingredients in a large bowl, toss to combine, pour into the roasting pan then place roast on top.

3. Cover tightly with aluminum foil then cut 4 small slits into the foil for steaming purposes.

4. Place the pan on the rack in the lower position then close the door.

5. Set the Vent Release Valve to SEAL, lower the Sealing Lever to the SEAL position and set the timer.

6. Set the oven to 450°F and function to ROAST.

7. Cook for 3 hours or until beef is very tender.

8. When cooking is complete, turn the Vent Release Valve to VENT and wait for all air to escape. Once vented, slowly raise the Sealing Lever and press the Door Release Button to open the door.

9. Remove, garnish as desired and serve.

Chicken Pot Pie

MAKES 4-6 SERVINGS

2 cups leftover chicken
1 small yellow onion, peeled and diced
1 large carrot, peeled and diced
1 celery stalk, diced
1 large Russet potato, peeled and cubed
1 cup frozen peas

1 can (10.75 ounces) cream of chicken soup
1 cup chicken stock
1/2 cup half & half
Kosher salt and fresh pepper to taste
1 frozen puff pastry sheet, thawed

1. Arrange the chicken in an even layer inside the roasting pan.

2. Scatter the onions, carrot, celery, potatoes and peas over the chicken in the pan.

3. In a mixing bowl combine the soup, stock, half & half, salt and pepper.

4. Pour soup mixture over the pan contents then top with the puff pastry sheet. Cut a hole in center to vent.

5. Place the pan on the rack in the lower position then close the door.

6. Set the Vent Release Valve to SEAL, lower the Sealing Lever to the SEAL position and set the timer.

7. Set the oven to 400°F and function to BAKE.

8. Cook for 40 minutes or until brown and bubbly.

9. When cooking is complete, turn the Vent Release Valve to VENT and wait for all air to escape. Once vented, slowly raise the Sealing Lever and press the Door Release Button to open the door.

10. Remove pan, garnish as desired and serve.

Easy No-Layer Sausage Lasagna

MAKES 6 SERVINGS

1 bag (9.6 ounces) precooked hearty sausage crumbles
1 medium yellow onion, chopped
4 garlic cloves, chopped
2 cups pasta sauce
1 teaspoon Italian seasoning
Kosher salt and fresh pepper to taste
1 1/2 cups beef stock
1/2 cup ricotta cheese
1/2 cup Parmesan cheese, grated
8 ounces dry pasta such as campanelle
1 bag (8 ounces) shredded Italian blend cheeses

1. In the roasting pan, combine all ingredients, except the Italian cheeses; stir to combine.

2. Cover tightly with aluminum foil then cut 4 small slits into the foil for steaming purposes.

3. Place the pan on the rack in the lower position then close the door.

4. Set the Vent Release Valve to SEAL, lower the Sealing Lever to the SEAL position and set the timer.

5. Set the oven to 450°F and function to BAKE.

6. Cook for 35 minutes.

7. When cooking is complete, turn the Vent Release Valve to VENT and wait for all air to escape. Once vented, slowly raise the Sealing Lever and press the Door Release Button to open the door.

8. Remove pan and scatter Italian cheese over the pan contents. Place back in the oven uncovered, repeat step 4 then cook for an additional 10 minutes or until cheese is melted, bubbly and is beginning to brown.

9. Remove, let stand for 10 minutes, garnish as desired and serve hot.

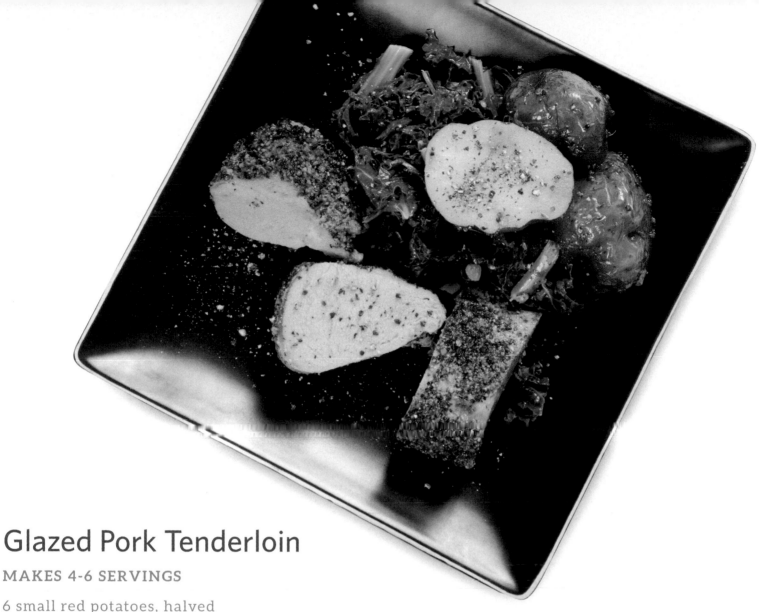

Glazed Pork Tenderloin

MAKES 4-6 SERVINGS

6 small red potatoes, halved
2 pork tenderloins (about 2 pounds)
2 tablespoons olive oil
1 tablespoon Montreal steak seasoning
2 tablespoons jarred apple jelly, softened

1. Place the potatoes and pork in the roasting pan.

2. In a small bowl combine the oil, steak seasoning and apple jelly. Brush mixture over the pork. Season potatoes with additional Montreal steak seasoning.

3. Place the pan on the rack in the lower position then close the door.

4. Set the Vent Release Valve to SEAL, lower the Sealing Lever to the SEAL position and set the timer.

5. Set the oven to 450°F and function to ROAST.

6. Cook for 25-35 minutes or until internal temperature of pork reaches 145°F on a meat thermometer.

7. When cooking is complete, turn the Vent Release Valve to VENT and wait for all air to escape. Once vented, slowly raise the Sealing Lever and press the Door Release Button to open the door.

8. Remove pan, garnish as desired and serve.

Triple Chocolate Chunk Brownies

MAKES 9 SERVINGS

1 cup (2 sticks) unsalted butter, melted
2 cups granulated sugar
4 large eggs
1/4 teaspoon kosher salt
1 teaspoon vanilla extract
1/2 cup cocoa powder
1 cup unbleached all purpose flour
1/2 cup each dark, milk and white chocolate chunks

1. In a mixing bowl, stir together the butter, sugar, eggs, salt and vanilla until smooth.

2. Add remaining ingredients and stir until no visible cocoa or flour remains. Grease the roasting pan then pour mixing bowl contents into pan.

3. Place the pan on the rack in the lower position then close the door.

4. Set the Vent Release Valve to SEAL, lower the Sealing Lever to the SEAL position and set the timer.

5. Set the oven to 325°F and function to BAKE.

6. Bake for 45 minutes or until a knife inserted off-center comes out with just a few moist crumbs clinging.

7. When cooking is complete, turn the Vent Release Valve to VENT and wait for all air to escape. Once vented, slowly raise the Sealing Lever and press the Door Release Button to open the door.

8. Remove brownies, garnish as desired and serve warm or at room temperature.

Wolf's Hong Kong White Fish

MAKES 4 SERVINGS

4 firm white fish fillets, such as cod or halibut
4 broccoli spears
1 tablespoon soy sauce + more for serving
4 teaspoons dark sesame oil
3 garlic cloves, julienned

1-inch piece of ginger, julienned
A handful of cilantro leaves, for serving
1 bunch green onions, sliced, for serving
1 tablespoon sesame seeds, for serving

1. Preheat the oven to 450°F, set the function to BAKE and timer to 10 minutes.

2. Place broil rack insert into drip/baking pan then apply nonstick cooking spray to the rack. Place fish and broccoli on rack. Drizzle with soy sauce and sesame oil then top with garlic and ginger.

3. Place the pan on the rack in the middle position then close the door.

4. Set the Vent Release Valve to SEAL, lower the Sealing Lever to the SEAL position and reset the timer.

5. Cook for 7-10 minutes or until fish is just turning opaque and flakes easily with a fork.

6. When cooking is complete, turn the Vent Release Valve to VENT and wait for all air to escape. Once vented, slowly raise the Sealing Lever and press the Door Release Button to open the door.

7. Remove fish, garnish as desired and serve topped with cilantro, green onions, sesame seeds and additional soy sauce.

TIP

For a leaner version, use a turkey breast instead of the pork. It won't be as juicy but will contain far less fat and the taste is still delicious.

Shredded Pork Carnitas

MAKES 6 SERVINGS

4 pounds pork shoulder, cut into large chunks
8 garlic cloves, minced
1 large white onion, sliced
Juice of 1 orange
2 tablespoons jarred chicken bouillon base or to taste
1 teaspoon ground cumin
1 teaspoon dried oregano
1/2 cup whole milk
1 cup water
Tortillas, cilantro and onions, for serving

1. Place all ingredients, except tortillas, cilantro and onions for serving, into the roasting pan.

2. Cover tightly with aluminum foil then cut 4 small slits into the foil for steaming purposes.

3. Place the pan on the rack in the lower position then close the door.

4. Set the Vent Release Valve to SEAL, lower the Sealing Lever to the SEAL position and set the timer.

5. Set the oven to 375°F and function to ROAST.

6. Roast for 3 hours or until meat is fall-apart tender.

7. When cooking is complete, turn the Vent Release Valve to VENT and wait for all air to escape. Once vented, slowly raise the Sealing Lever and press the Door Release Button to open the door.

8. Remove meat from pan, skim off excess fat then shred using tongs and return to sauce in pan.

9. Garnish as desired and serve with tortillas, cilantro and onions.

Roasted Chicken Soup

MAKES 6 SERVINGS

1 leftover chicken or turkey carcass (from recipe on page 6, 80, 114 or 125)
10 cups chicken stock
1 medium onion, chopped
2 carrots, chopped
3 celery stalks, chopped
1 medium tomato, chopped
3 sprigs fresh thyme
3 cups leftover chicken or turkey (from recipe on page 6, 80, 114 or 125)
Kosher salt and fresh pepper to taste
2 cups dry pasta
Handful of fresh dill or parsley, for serving

1. Combine the carcass and chicken stock in a stockpot, breaking the carcass if needed to submerge under broth.

2. Bring to a boil over high heat then reduce heat to low and simmer for 1 hour.

3. Pull out the carcass and discard. Run a strainer around the stockpot to catch any stray bits.

4. Add remaining ingredients, except pasta and dill/parsley, then bring back to a simmer.

5. Cook for 30 minutes then add the pasta and cook for an additional 10-15 minutes or until pasta is tender.

6. Garnish as desired and serve with dill or parsley.

―――――― TIP ――――――

Use all egg whites, skip the
sugar and use sugar-free
ketchup or tomato paste if
you prefer a leaner loaf.

Mom's Turkey Meatloaf

MAKES 4-5 SERVINGS

1 pound lean ground turkey
2 large eggs
1/4 cup whole milk
1/2 cup dry oatmeal
1/2 cup ketchup + more for the top

1 large yellow onion, chopped
1/2 cup ricotta cheese
1 teaspoon poultry seasoning
Kosher salt and fresh pepper to taste
1 tablespoon brown sugar, packed

1. In a large mixing bowl, combine all ingredients, except brown sugar, until blended.

2. Mound into an oblong loaf shape in the roasting pan, top with additional ketchup then sprinkle with brown sugar.

3. Place the pan on the rack in the lower position then close the door.

4. Set the Vent Release Valve to SEAL, lower the Sealing Lever to the SEAL position and set the timer.

5. Set the oven to 350°F and function to BAKE.

6. Cook for 45 minutes or until well-browned and internal temperature reaches 165°F on a meat thermometer.

7. When cooking is complete, turn the Vent Release Valve to VENT and wait for all air to escape. Once vented, slowly raise the Sealing Lever and press the Door Release Button to open the door.

8. Remove meatloaf, garnish as desired and serve.

Key Lime Pie

MAKES 1 PIE

For the Pie:
1 can (14 ounces) sweetened condensed milk
4 large egg yolks
1 tablespoon fresh lime zest
1/2 cup fresh lime juice (about 6 limes)
1-2 drops green food coloring (optional)
1 prepared pie crust, baked

For the Meringue:
4 large egg whites
1/2 cup granulated sugar

1. Preheat the oven to 350°F, set the function to BAKE and timer to 10 minutes (you will not be using pressure for this recipe).

2. In a bowl, whisk together all pie ingredients, except crust, until smooth then pour into prepared pie crust in pie pan.

3. Place the pan on the rack in the middle position then close the door and reset timer.

4. Bake for 20 minutes or until custard is just set then remove and let cool.

5. Combine the meringue ingredients in a clean bowl. Using a hand mixer with clean beaters, beat on high for 3-4 minutes or until stiff peaks form.

6. Decoratively swirl meringue on top of the pie using a spoon.

7. Reset oven to 450°F, function to BROIL then place baking rack in lower position.

8. Broil pie for 5 minutes or until edges are browned.

9. Remove, chill then cut into wedges and serve.

Fajitas

MAKES 2-4 SERVINGS

1 bell pepper, sliced
1 small white onion, sliced
Fajita seasoning mix or Mexican seasoning to taste
1 skirt steak (about 1 pound)
2 tablespoons canola oil
Tortillas and desired condiments, for serving

TIP

You can substitute 2 chicken breasts for the beef but increase the broil time by 5 minutes or until internal temperature reaches 165°F on a meat thermometer when measured at the thickest part of the breasts.

1. Preheat the oven to 450°F, set the function to BROIL and timer to 10 minutes.

2. Place peppers and onions on the drip/baking pan then sprinkle with fajita seasoning.

3. Season both sides of the skirt steak with fajita seasoning, place on broiler rack (cut steak in half if it is too long for the rack) then fit the rack with the steak over the top of the vegetables in the drip/baking pan.

4. Drizzle oil over the vegetables and steak.

5. Place the pan on the rack in the upper position then close the door.

6. Set the Vent Release Valve to SEAL, lower the Sealing Lever to the SEAL position and reset the timer.

7. Broil for 8 minutes then turn the Vent Release Valve to VENT and wait for all air to escape. Once vented, slowly raise the Sealing Lever and press the Door Release Button to open the door.

8. Turn the meat over, repeat step 6 then broil for an additional 5-6 minutes or until desired doneness is reached.

9. Remove steak, slice into thin strips then serve with peppers, onions, tortillas and condiments of your choice.

Stuffing Stuffed Pork Loin

MAKES 6 SERVINGS

1 pork loin (3-4 pounds)
Kosher salt and fresh pepper to taste
2 cups prepared stuffing + more for serving

2 tablespoons soy sauce
1 tablespoon olive oil
1 tablespoon honey

1. Cut the pork loin down the middle, but not quite through, so that it opens like a book.

2. Season liberally with salt and pepper then place some stuffing along the center.

3. Close the sides of the pork loin together then tie using kitchen string at intervals.

4. Season with salt and pepper then mix together the soy sauce, oil and honey. Brush soy mixture all over the pork then place it in the roasting pan.

5. Place the pan on the rack in the lower position then close the door.

6. Set the Vent Release Valve to SEAL, lower the Sealing Lever to the SEAL position and set the timer.

7. Set the oven to 450°F and function to ROAST.

8. Cook for 1 hour or until internal temperature registers 155°F on a meat thermometer.

9. When cooking is complete, turn the Vent Release Valve to VENT and wait for all air to escape. Once vented, slowly raise the Sealing Lever and press the Door Release Button to open the door.

10. Remove pork, let rest for 10 minutes then garnish as desired and serve with additional stuffing.

Bacon, Egg and Bagel Bake

MAKES 4 SERVINGS

4 small bagels of your choice
6 bacon slices, cooked and crumbled
1 small tomato, chopped
4 green onions, sliced
1/2 cup Swiss cheese, shredded
1/4 cup Parmesan cheese, grated
4 large eggs
Kosher salt and fresh pepper to taste
2 teaspoons apple cider vinegar
1 1/2 cups half & half or milk
1 package (8 ounces) cream cheese

1. Cut bagels into small pieces then transfer to the roasting pan.

2. Scatter bacon, tomatoes, green onions, Swiss and Parmesan cheeses over the bagel pieces.

3. In a large bowl, whisk together the eggs, salt, pepper, vinegar and half & half then pour mixture evenly over the pan contents.

4. Dot the surface of the pan contents with teaspoon-size bits of cream cheese then cover with plastic wrap and refrigerate for a minimum of 1 hour or up to 24 hours to allow the bagels to soak up the liquid.

5. Place the pan on the rack in the lower position then close the door.

6. Set the Vent Release Valve to SEAL, lower the Sealing Lever to the SEAL position and set the timer.

7. Set the oven to 350°F and function to BAKE.

8. Cook for 40 minutes or until puffed and well browned. A knife inserted off-center should come out clean.

9. When cooking is complete, turn the Vent Release Valve to VENT and wait for all air to escape. Once vented, slowly raise the Sealing Lever and press the Door Release Button to open the door.

10. Remove pan, garnish as desired and serve.

TIP

This is a great recipe to make using stale bagels. You can also use cinnamon raisin or blueberry bagels to achieve a sweet and salty contrast.

Gluten-Free Corn Bread

MAKES ONE 8-INCH ROUND

1 large egg
1 1/4 cups buttermilk
1/2 cup unsalted butter, melted
1/2 cup corn, fresh, frozen, or canned
1/2 cup rice flour
1/2 cup potato starch flour

2 teaspoons xanthan gum
1 teaspoon baking soda
1/2 teaspoon baking powder
2 teaspoons kosher salt
1/4 cup granulated sugar

1. Apply nonstick cooking spray to an 8-inch round pan; set aside.

2. In a mixing bowl whisk together the egg, buttermilk, butter and corn.

3. In a separate mixing bowl stir together the remaining ingredients until blended.

4. Whisk the dry ingredients into the wet ingredients then pour into the round pan.

5. Place the pan on the rack in the lower position then close the door.

6. Set the Vent Release Valve to SEAL, lower the Sealing Lever to the SEAL position and set the timer.

7. Set the oven to 350°F and function to BAKE.

8. Bake for 30 minutes or until golden brown and a wooden pick inserted off-center comes out with just a few moist crumbs clinging to it.

9. When cooking is complete, turn the Vent Release Valve to VENT and wait for all air to escape. Once vented, slowly raise the Sealing Lever and press the Door Release Button to open the door.

10. Remove cornbread, garnish as desired and serve.

TIP

Best served over the Oven Steamed Rice on page 104 or Baked Brown Rice on page 75.

One Pan Swiss Steak

MAKES 4 SERVINGS

1 pound cubed steaks (tenderized)
1 large yellow onion, sliced
1 green bell pepper, sliced
1 celery stalk, sliced
1 carrot, sliced
3 garlic cloves, chopped

2 cups canned tomato puree
2 tablespoons all purpose flour
Kosher salt and fresh pepper to taste
1 tablespoon jarred beef bouillon base or to taste
2 tablespoons bottled steak sauce

1. Place the meat, onions, bell peppers, celery, carrots and garlic into the roasting pan.

2. In a bowl, whisk together remaining ingredients until smooth, pour evenly over the pan contents, cover tightly with aluminum foil then cut 4 small slits into the foil for steaming purposes.

3. Place the pan on the rack in the lower position then close the door.

4. Set the Vent Release Valve to SEAL, lower the Sealing Lever to the SEAL position and set the timer.

5. Set the oven to 400°F and function to BAKE.

6. Cook for 1 1/2 hours or until fall-apart tender.

7. When cooking is complete, turn the Vent Release Valve to VENT and wait for all air to escape. Once vented, slowly raise the Sealing Lever and press the Door Release Button to open the door.

8. Remove pan, garnish as desired and serve.

Chicken Pesto Pasta

MAKES 4 SERVINGS

2 cups leftover chicken or turkey
1/2 cup jarred pesto
1/4 teaspoon chili flakes
2 cups chicken stock

1/2 cup olives
1/2 cup ricotta cheese + more for serving
8 ounces dry pasta
1 cup Italian blend cheese, shredded

1. Combine all ingredients, except Italian blend cheese, in the roasting pan.

2. Cover tightly with aluminum foil then cut 4 small slits into the foil for steaming purposes.

3. Place the pan on the rack in the lower position then close the door.

4. Set the Vent Release Valve to SEAL, lower the Sealing Lever to the SEAL position and set the timer.

5. Set the oven to 400°F and function to BAKE.

6. Cook for 40 minutes.

7. When cooking is complete, turn the Vent Release Valve to VENT and wait for all air to escape. Once vented, slowly raise the Sealing Lever and press the Door Release Button to open the door.

8. Remove pan and discard foil. Stir, sprinkle the cheese over the pan contents, repeat step 4 and cook for an additional 10 minutes.

9. Remove pasta, garnish as desired and serve.

TIP

If you do not have a large-size muffin tin, you can use ramekins or other small oven-safe dishes.

Easy Crust Egg Cups

MAKES 6 CUPS

6 sandwich bread slices
Unsalted butter, softened, for spreading
6 slices Canadian bacon
6 large eggs

1/2 cup Swiss or Cheddar cheese, grated
1 green onion, sliced
Kosher salt and fresh pepper to taste

1. Apply nonstick cooking spray to a large-size 6-spot muffin tin.

2. Butter one side of each bread slice then press buttered-side down into each well.

3. Tuck Canadian bacon slices down on top of the bread in each well then top with an egg, some grated cheese, greens onions, salt and pepper.

4. Place the pan on the rack in the lower position then close the door.

5. Set the Vent Release Valve to SEAL, lower the Sealing Lever to the SEAL position and set the timer.

6. Set the oven to 375°F and function to BAKE.

7. Cook for 20 minutes or until eggs are puffed and edges of bread are turning brown.

8. When cooking is complete, turn the Vent Release Valve to VENT and wait for all air to escape. Once vented, slowly raise the Sealing Lever and press the Door Release Button to open the door.

9. Use a spatula to remove cups from muffin tin, garnish as desired and serve hot.

Buffalo Shrimp

MAKES 4 SERVINGS

2 pounds small shrimp, tails removed
1 cup bottled wing sauce
1/2 cup heavy cream
1/2 cup blue cheese, crumbled
1/2 cup panko breadcrumbs

1. Preheat the oven to 450°F, set the function to ROAST and timer to 10 minutes.

2. Place the shrimp, wing sauce and cream into the roasting pan and stir.

3. Scatter the blue cheese over the pan contents then sprinkle the breadcrumbs over the cheese.

4. Place the pan on the rack in the lower position then close the door.

5. Set the Vent Release Valve to SEAL, lower the Sealing Lever to the SEAL position and reset the timer.

6. Cook for 20 minutes or until breadcrumbs are brown and sauce is bubbly.

7. When cooking is complete, turn the Vent Release Valve to VENT and wait for all air to escape. Once vented, slowly raise the Sealing Lever and press the Door Release Button to open the door.

8. Remove shrimp, garnish as desired and serve.

—— TIP ——

Combining all ingredients in
the bowl allows for the use
of less oil.

Best Roast Vegetables

MAKES 4 SERVINGS

6 small red potatoes, cut into quarters
2 carrots, peeled then cut lengthwise
1 parsnip, peeled then cut lengthwise
1 large white onion, cut into chunks
1 celery stalk, cut into chunks
1 tablespoon olive oil

1 tablespoon unsalted butter, melted
1 teaspoon apple cider vinegar
1 tablespoon kosher salt or to taste
1 teaspoon black pepper
A few sprigs fresh thyme, sage or rosemary

1. Place all ingredients into a large bowl, toss well then transfer bowl contents to the roasting pan.

2. Place the pan on the rack in the lower position then close the door.

3. Set the Vent Release Valve to SEAL, lower the Sealing Lever to the SEAL position and set the timer.

4. Set the oven to 450°F and function to ROAST.

5. Cook for 40 minutes or until vegetables are deeply browned, fork tender and fragrant.

6. When cooking is complete, turn the Vent Release Valve to VENT and wait for all air to escape. Once vented, slowly raise the Sealing Lever and press the Door Release Button to open the door.

7. Remove vegetables, garnish as desired and serve.

Bacon Wrapped Meatloaf

MAKES 4-5 SERVINGS

1 pound ground beef
1 large egg
1/2 cup soda crackers, crumbled
1/4 cup bottled BBQ sauce
1/4 cup ketchup
2 tablespoons whole milk
1 small yellow onion, chopped
1 teaspoon dried sage
2 teaspoons kosher salt or to taste
1/2 teaspoon freshly cracked pepper
8 bacon or turkey-bacon slices

1. In a large mixing bowl, gently combine the beef, egg, crackers, BBQ sauce, ketchup, milk, onion, sage, salt and pepper; do not over mix.

2. Lay a larger piece of plastic wrap on the counter and arrange the bacon slices on it in an overlapping fashion. Place beef mixture in an oval shape in the center of the bacon slices. Fold each bacon slice up and over the top of the loaf.

3. Apply nonstick cooking spray to the roasting pan then lift loaf by the plastic wrap and flip over into the pan so that the bacon ends are underneath.

4. Place on the rack in the lower position then close the door.

5. Set the Vent Release Valve to SEAL, lower the Sealing Lever to the SEAL position and set the timer.

6. Set the oven to 350°F and function to BAKE.

7. Cook for 30-40 minutes or until internal temperature registers 165°F on a meat thermometer.

8. When cooking is complete, turn the Vent Release Valve to VENT and wait for all air to escape. Once vented, slowly raise the Sealing Lever and press the Door Release Button to open the door.

9. Remove loaf, garnish as desired and serve with additional ketchup or BBQ sauce.

TIP

If you don't like BBQ sauce, you can use your favorite pasta sauce instead.

Wolf's Spicy Shrimp Pizza

MAKES 2 SERVINGS

1 store-bought pizza dough ball (8 ounces)
All purpose flour, for the dough
2 tablespoons jarred pesto
1 cup mozzarella cheese, shredded

2 tablespoons Parmesan cheese, grated
1 cup raw shrimp, sliced (butterflied)
Kosher salt and fresh pepper to taste
Chili flakes to taste

1. Preheat the oven to 450°F, set the function to BAKE and timer to 10 minutes.

2. Stretch dough into a rough rectangle or desired shape using flour to prevent sticking then place in roasting pan or on a pizza screen.

3. Spread the pesto over the dough then top with the cheeses and shrimp then season with salt, pepper and chili flakes.

4. Place the pan on the rack in the middle position then close the door.

5. Set the Vent Release Valve to SEAL, lower the Sealing Lever to the SEAL position and reset the timer.

6. Cook for 7-10 minutes or until well browned and bubbly. Turn pizza around halfway through cooking if desired.

7. When cooking is complete, turn the Vent Release Valve to VENT and wait for all air to escape. Once vented, slowly raise the Sealing Lever and press the Door Release Button to open the door.

8. Remove pizza, garnish as desired and serve.

Brats, Peppers and Onion Hoagie

MAKES 4 SERVINGS

2 bell peppers, sliced
1/2 cup jarred Italian hot peppers, drained and sliced
1 large yellow onion, sliced
4 Italian sausages (8 ounces each)
A few sprigs fresh oregano
2 tablespoons olive oil
Kosher salt and fresh pepper to taste
4 hoagie buns, for serving

1. Place the peppers and onions on drip/baking pan then place the sausages on top.

2. Scatter the oregano around the sausages. Drizzle pan contents with oil then season with salt and pepper.

3. Place the pan on the rack in the lower position then close the door.

4. Set the Vent Release Valve to SEAL, lower the Sealing Lever to the SEAL position and set the timer.

5. Set the oven to 450°F and function to ROAST.

6. Cook for 35 minutes or until sausages are well browned and internal temperature is 165°F on a meat thermometer.

7. When cooking is complete, turn the Vent Release Valve to VENT and wait for all air to escape. Once vented, slowly raise the Sealing Lever and press the Door Release Button to open the door.

8. Remove sausages and serve on buns with a spoonful of the flavorful pan juices drizzled on top.

Broiled Hot Dogs

MAKES 4 SERVINGS

4 large hot dogs
2 American cheese slices
4 hotdog buns
Condiments of choice

1. Using a knife, cut a slit into each hot dog lengthwise (do not cut all the way through) then place them on one side of the drip/baking pan.

2. Cut cheese slices into 4 strips lengthwise then tuck 2 cheese strips into each hot dog slit.

3. Place the pan on the rack in the upper position then close the door.

4. Set the Vent Release Valve to SEAL, lower the Sealing Lever to the SEAL position and set the timer.

5. Set the oven to 450°F and function to BROIL.

6. Cook for 8 minutes or just until hot dogs begin to brown along edges and cheese is melted.

7. When cooking is complete, turn the Vent Release Valve to VENT and wait for all air to escape. Once vented, slowly raise the Sealing Lever and press the Door Release Button to open the door.

8. Remove hot dogs, garnish as desired and serve with condiments of your choice.

Braised Pork and Apples

MAKES 4 SERVINGS

2 pounds pork shoulder or chops
2 Granny Smith apples, thickly sliced
2 tablespoons jarred chicken bouillon or to taste
2 teaspoons dried sage
1 large yellow onion, thickly sliced
3 garlic cloves

1/3 cup light brown sugar, packed
2 cups apple cider or juice
1 tablespoon apple cider vinegar
1/4 cup unsalted butter
Kosher salt and fresh pepper to taste

1. Combine all ingredients in the roasting pan.

2. Cover tightly with aluminum foil then cut 4 small slits into the foil for steaming purposes.

3. Place the pan on the rack in the lower position then close the door.

4. Set the Vent Release Valve to SEAL, lower the Sealing Lever to the SEAL position and set the timer.

5. Set the oven to 450°F and function to ROAST.

6. Cook for 3 hours or until meat is fall-apart tender.

7. When cooking is complete, turn the Vent Release Valve to VENT and wait for all air to escape. Once vented, slowly raise the Sealing Lever and press the Door Release Button to open the door.

8. Remove pork then skim off excess fat using a spoon.

9. Garnish as desired and serve.

Baked Rice Pudding

MAKES 6-8 SERVINGS

2 cups short-grain white rice
3 1/2 cups water
1 tablespoon vanilla extract
2 teaspoons ground cinnamon
1/2 teaspoon kosher salt or to taste
1 teaspoon apple cider vinegar
1/2 cup granulated sugar or other sweetener
1/2 cup raisins
1 1/2 cups half & half or milk

1. Line the roasting pan with heavy-duty aluminum foil.

2. Combine all ingredients except half & half or milk in the pan and stir gently.

3. Tightly cover pan with aluminum foil and cut 4 small slits into the foil for steaming purposes.

4. Place the pan on the rack in the lower position then close the door.

5. Set the Vent Release Valve to SEAL, lower the Sealing Lever to the SEAL position and set the timer.

6. Set the oven to 450°F, function to BAKE.

7. Cook for 35 minutes.

8. When cooking is complete, turn the Vent Release Valve to VENT and wait for all air to escape. Once vented, slowly raise the Sealing Lever and press the Door Release Button to open the door.

9. Remove pan, discard the foil then stir in the half & half or milk until blended. If you prefer your rice pudding looser, add more half & half or milk, it thickens while standing.

10. Add more sugar if desired, garnish as desired and serve.

TIP

Do not add the half & half or milk with the other ingredients before cooking as it will boil over in the oven when you release the pressure. It also curdles during the intense heat of the pressure oven so only add it after cooking is completed and pan is out of the oven.

Best Buffalo Wings

MAKES 4-6 SERVINGS

18 small chicken wings (about 3 pounds)
2 tablespoons unsalted butter, melted
Kosher salt and fresh pepper to taste
1 cup bottled wing sauce

1/4 cup blue cheese crumbles
Ranch or blue cheese dressing, for dipping
Celery sticks, for serving

1. Preheat the oven to 450°F, set the function to BAKE and timer to 10 minutes.

2. In the roasting pan, toss together the wings, butter, salt, pepper and wing sauce.

3. Place the pan on the rack in the lower position then close the door.

4. Set the Vent Release Valve to SEAL, lower the Sealing Lever to the SEAL position and reset the timer.

5. Cook for 10 minutes then switch function to BROIL and cook for an additional 10 minutes. Cook until the thickest part of the wings register 165°F on a meat thermometer.

6. When cooking is complete, turn the Vent Release Valve to VENT and wait for all air to escape. Once vented, slowly raise the Sealing Lever and press the Door Release Button to open the door.

7. Remove wings, garnish as desired then serve with blue cheese crumbles, dressing and celery.

Broiled Lamb Chops

MAKES 4 SERVINGS

8 small lamb rib chops
Kosher salt and fresh pepper to taste
1/4 cup jarred pesto

1. Preheat the oven to 450°F, set the function to BROIL and timer to 10 minutes.

2. Season lamb chops with salt and pepper then place on the drip/baking pan with broil rack insert.

3. Brush the top of each chop with pesto.

4. Place the pan on the rack in the upper position then close the door.

5. Set the Vent Release Valve to SEAL, lower the Sealing Lever to the SEAL position and reset the timer.

6. Cook for 5-6 minutes then turn the Vent Release Valve to VENT and wait for all air to escape. Once vented, slowly raise the Sealing Lever and press the Door Release Button to open the door.

7. Remove pan, turn each chop over using tongs then top with remaining pesto and place back in the oven.

8. Repeat step 5 then cook for an additional 5-6 minutes or until desired doneness is achieved. Remove, garnish as desired and serve.

Cheesy Goodness Popovers

MAKES 6 SERVINGS

3/4 cup whole milk

3 large eggs

2 teaspoons powdered sugar

1 teaspoon kosher salt

3/4 cup all purpose flour

2 tablespoons Parmesan cheese, grated

6 teaspoons vegetable oil + more for muffin tin

3 tablespoons long shredded Parmesan cheese

--- TIP ---

Allowing to let the batter rest for 1 hour at room temperature prior to baking will result in taller popovers.

1. Place all ingredients, except long shredded Parmesan, into a blender. Process for 30 seconds or until smooth then let stand at room temperature for a minimum of 1 hour until ready to use.

2. Preheat the oven to 450°F, set the function to BAKE and timer to 10 minutes.

3. Drop a teaspoon of oil into each well of a 6-spot muffin tin then place in the oven on the rack in the lower position for 5 minutes to heat.

4. Remove pan, pour the room temperature batter into each well until each is almost full then top with some of the long shredded Parmesan cheese. Return to oven.

5. Set the Vent Release Valve to SEAL, lower the Sealing Lever to the SEAL position and reset the timer.

6. Bake for about 30 minutes or until popovers have grown to be a few inches taller than the pan and are a deep brown color.

7. When cooking is complete, turn the Vent Release Valve to VENT and wait for all air to escape. Once vented, slowly raise the Sealing Lever and press the Door Release Button to open the door.

8. Remove and serve immediately before they begin to deflate.

Best Beef Brisket

MAKES 4 SERVINGS

3-4 pounds beef brisket, trimmed
Kosher salt and fresh pepper to taste
1 3/4 cups beef stock
2 tablespoons tomato paste
1/2 cup light brown sugar, packed
1/3 cup inexpensive balsamic vinegar
1 tablespoon paprika
2 tablespoons onion powder
1 teaspoon garlic powder

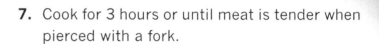

1. Place the brisket fat-side up into the roasting pan.

2. In a bowl, whisk together remaining ingredients then pour over the brisket.

3. Cover tightly with aluminum foil then cut 4 small slits into the foil for steaming purposes.

4. Place the pan on the rack in the lower position then close the door.

5. Set the Vent Release Valve to SEAL, lower the Sealing Lever to the SEAL position and set the timer.

6. Set the oven to 325°F and function to ROAST.

7. Cook for 3 hours or until meat is tender when pierced with a fork.

8. When cooking is complete, turn the Vent Release Valve to VENT and wait for all air to escape. Once vented, slowly raise the Sealing Lever and press the Door Release Button to open the door.

9. Remove pan then transfer brisket to a cutting board.

10. Cut into desired slices across the grain, starting at the pointed end.

11. Dip slices in the sauce at the bottom of the roasting pan, garnish as desired and serve.

TIP

To make a complete meal, add chunks of potatoes, carrots and onions to the pan before adding the brisket. The vegetables will be very soft but completely delicious.

Broiled Patty Melt

MAKES 4 SERVINGS

2 pounds ground beef (80% lean)
1/2 cup sharp Cheddar cheese, cut into small cubes
2 teaspoons jarred beef bouillon base or to taste
Kosher salt and fresh pepper to taste
4 Cheddar cheese slices
Buns and condiments, for serving

1. Preheat the oven to 450°F, set the function to BROIL and timer to 10 minutes.

2. In a mixing bowl, gently combine the beef, cheese cubes, bouillon base, salt and pepper.

3. Form mixture into four 1-inch thick patties then place on the drip/baking pan with broil rack insert.

4. Place the pan on the rack in the upper position then close the door.

5. Set the Vent Release Valve to SEAL, lower the Sealing Lever to the SEAL position and reset the timer.

6. Cook for 8 minutes then turn the Vent Release Valve to VENT and wait for all air to escape. Once vented, slowly raise the Sealing Lever and press the Door Release Button to open the door.

7. Remove pan, flip each patty over, reset timer then broil for an additional 5-8 minutes. Top each patty with a slice of cheese and broil for an additional 2-3 minutes or until melted.

8. Remove patty melt, garnish as desired and serve with buns and condiments of your choice.

Broiled Salmon with Avocado Salsa

MAKES 4 SERVINGS

4 salmon fillets (6 ounces each)
1 tablespoon olive oil
2 teaspoons honey
Kosher salt and fresh pepper to taste

1 avocado, diced
2 teaspoons lime juice
1 tablespoon cilantro leaves
2 small cherry tomatoes, chopped

1. Preheat the oven to 450°F, set the function to BROIL and timer to 10 minutes.

2. Brush salmon with oil and honey then season with salt and pepper.

3. Place broil rack insert into drip/baking pan, apply nonstick cooking spray to the rack then place salmon on rack.

4. Place the pan on the rack in the upper position then close the door.

5. Set the Vent Release Valve to SEAL, lower the Sealing Lever to the SEAL position and reset the timer.

6. Cook for 10 minutes or until just opaque and cooked through.

7. While salmon is cooking, toss the avocado, lime juice, cilantro, cherry tomatoes and a pinch of salt in a medium bowl; set aside until salmon is done cooking.

8. When cooking is complete, turn the Vent Release Valve to VENT and wait for all air to escape. Once vented, slowly raise the Sealing Lever and press the Door Release Button to open the door.

9. Remove salmon, garnish as desired and serve with avocado salsa.

Chocolate Chunk Cookies

MAKES 24 SERVINGS

1 cup unsalted butter, softened
1 cup granulated sugar
1/2 cup light brown sugar, packed
2 cups all purpose flour
1 teaspoon baking soda
1 teaspoon kosher salt
2 teaspoons vanilla extract
2 large eggs
1 cup semi-sweet chocolate chunks
1 cup white chocolate chunks
1 cup milk chocolate chunks

TIP

If you prefer chewy cookies, as soon as you remove a cookie sheet from the oven, grasp it with potholders and rap the pan flat down on the counter twice. This will slightly deflate the cookies and greatly improve the chewy texture.

1. In a large mixing bowl, cream the butter using a hand mixer then add each ingredient in the order listed, mixing well after each addition.

2. Preheat the oven to 350°F, set the function to BAKE and timer to 10 minutes.

3. Drop 6 mounds (2 tablespoons each) onto the foil or parchment-lined drip/baking pan.

4. Place the pan on the rack in the lower position then close the door.

5. Set the Vent Release Valve to SEAL, lower the Sealing Lever to the SEAL position and reset the timer.

6. Bake for 12-15 minutes or until golden in color, rotating pan around halfway through baking.

7. When cooking is complete, turn the Vent Release Valve to VENT and wait for all air to escape. Once vented, slowly raise the Sealing Lever and press the Door Release Button to open the door.

8. Remove cookies, repeat with remaining dough and serve.

Buffalo Chicken Dip

MAKES 6 SERVINGS

2 cups leftover chicken or turkey, diced
2 packages (8 ounces each) cream cheese, softened
1 cup bottled ranch or blue cheese dressing
1/2 cup blue cheese crumbles
2 cups sharp Cheddar cheese, grated
1 cup bottled Buffalo wing sauce
1 bunch green onions, sliced
1 cup panko or breadcrumbs
Crackers, for serving

1. In a mixing bowl combine all ingredients except panko and ingredients for serving.

2. Apply nonstick cooking spray to the roasting pan, add the mixing bowl contents then scatter the panko evenly over the top.

3. Place the pan on the rack in the lower position then close the door.

4. Set the Vent Release Valve to SEAL, lower the Sealing Lever to the SEAL position and set the timer.

5. Set the oven to 350°F and function to BAKE.

6. Cook for 25 minutes or until brown and bubbly.

7. When cooking is complete, turn the Vent Release Valve to VENT and wait for all air to escape. Once vented, slowly raise the Sealing Lever and press the Door Release Button to open the door.

8. Remove, garnish as desired and serve with crackers.

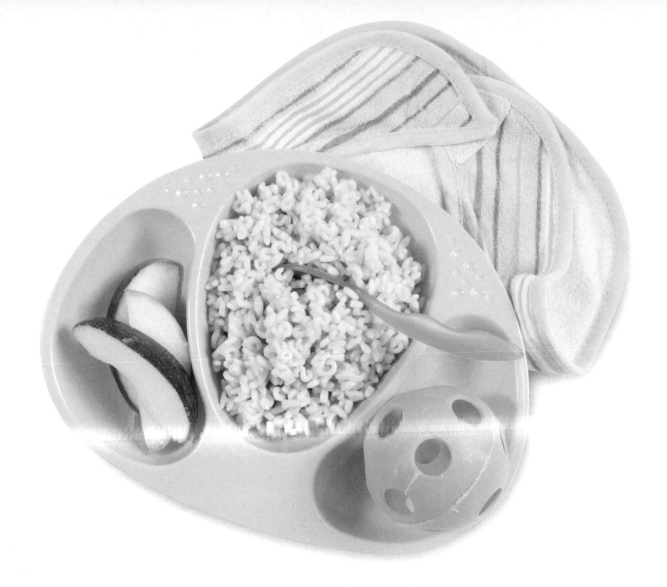

Buttered Oven Noodles

MAKES 4 SERVINGS

2 cups small pasta, dry
3 cups water or stock (if using water add some kosher salt to taste)
2 tablespoons unsalted butter

1. Combine all ingredients in the roasting pan.

2. Cover tightly with aluminum foil then cut 4 small slits into the foil for steaming purposes.

3. Place the pan on the rack in the lower position then close the door.

4. Set the Vent Release Valve to SEAL, lower the Sealing Lever to the SEAL position and set the timer.

5. Set the oven to 450°F and function to BAKE.

6. Cook for 25 minutes.

7. When cooking is complete, turn the Vent Release Valve to VENT and wait for all air to escape. Once vented, slowly raise the Sealing Lever and press the Door Release Button to open the door.

8. Remove noodles, stir using a spatula, garnish as desired and serve.

Braised Lamb Shanks

MAKES 4 SERVINGS

4 lamb shanks
1 tablespoon jarred beef bouillon base or to taste
Kosher salt and fresh pepper to taste
1 tablespoon paprika
12 whole garlic cloves
A few sprigs fresh rosemary
2 large yellow onions, chopped
2 large carrots, chopped
1 cup mixed olives
1 can (28 ounces) tomato puree
Fresh rosemary, for serving

1. Using gloves, rub the shanks with the bouillon base paste all over then season with salt, pepper and paprika (this will take the place of searing the shanks).

2. Place remaining ingredients, except rosemary for serving, in the roasting pan and stir.

3. Place lamb shanks on top of the pan contents. Cover tightly with aluminum foil then cut 4 small slits into the foil for steaming purposes.

4. Place the pan on the rack in the lower position then close the door.

5. Set the Vent Release Valve to SEAL, lower the Sealing Lever to the SEAL position and set the timer.

6. Set the oven to 375°F and function to ROAST.

7. Cook for 70 minutes or until meat is fall-apart tender and sauce is bubbly.

8. When cooking is complete, turn the Vent Release Valve to VENT and wait for all air to escape. Once vented, slowly raise the Sealing Lever and press the Door Release Button to open the door.

9. Remove lamb, garnish as desired, top with rosemary and serve.

TIP

The traditional way of making this dish involves searing the lamb shanks. The method in this recipe skips the searing without compromising the taste thanks to the infusion flavor technology of the pressure oven.

Centerpiece Stuffed Squash

MAKES 4-6 SERVINGS

2 acorn squash, butternut squash or pumpkins
Kosher salt and fresh pepper to taste
4 tablespoons unsalted butter, melted
1 medium yellow onion, diced
2 cups Italian bread, torn
1 cup Swiss cheese, shredded
1/2 cup Parmesan cheese, grated
3 large cggs, beaten
1 cup half & half or heavy cream
1 cup fresh kale, chopped

1. Cut off the tops from the squash then scrape out all the seeds using a spoon; reserve tops.

2. Season the inside as well as the underside of the top of the squash with salt and pepper.

3. In a mixing bowl, stir together remaining ingredients then spoon mixture into squash.

4. Place squash and cut off tops in the roasting pan.

5. Place the pan on the rack in the lower position then close the door.

6. Set the Vent Release Valve to SEAL, lower the Sealing Lever to the SEAL position and set the timer.

7. Set the oven to 400°F and function to BAKE.

8. Cook for 70 minutes or until squash contents are bubbly and squash is tender when pierced with a knife.

9. When cooking is complete, turn the Vent Release Valve to VENT and wait for all air to escape. Once vented, slowly raise the Sealing Lever and press the Door Release Button to open the door.

10. Remove squash and let cool for 10 minutes.

11. Garnish as desired and serve.

TIP

Loosely cover with aluminum foil if squash begins to brown too soon which largely depends on how tall your squash is.

Butterflied Whole Turkey

MAKES 8 SERVINGS

1 turkey (10 pounds), thawed
1 tablespoon olive oil
Kosher salt and fresh pepper to taste
2 tablespoons soy sauce
2 teaspoons honey

1. Remove turkey from refrigerator. If desired, for a crispier skin and more even cooking, let the turkey rest at room temperature for 1 to 1 1/2 hours. Otherwise proceed to next step.

2. Preheat the oven to 450°F, set the function to ROAST and timer to 10 minutes.

3. Use sturdy scissors (and gloves if you prefer) to cut down either side of the backbone then completely remove it. You can use either side of the tail as a guide for where to start snipping or ask your butcher to do this for you.

4. Turn turkey over, breast-side up, and press firmly down on the breast to flatten it.

5. Dry turkey off using paper towels and place it in the roasting pan.

6. Rub turkey with oil then season with salt and pepper.

7. Place the pan on the rack in the lower position then close the door.

8. Set the Vent Release Valve to SEAL, lower the Sealing Lever to the SEAL position and reset the timer.

9. Roast turkey for 30 minutes.

10. While turkey is roasting, thoroughly stir together the soy sauce and honey in a small bowl.

11. When cooking is complete, turn the Vent Release Valve to VENT and wait for all air to escape. Once vented, slowly raise the Sealing Lever and press the Door Release Button to open the door.

12. Remove pan then brush the soy sauce mixture all over the turkey skin.

13. Return to oven, repeat step 8 then cook for an additional 15 minutes or until brown and thigh registers 165°F on a meat thermometer.

14. Remove from oven, let rest for 10 minutes then garnish as desired and serve.

---- TIP ----

Leftovers are great for making the
BBQ Chicken Pizza on page 10, Buffalo
Chicken Dip on page 62, Chicken and
Broccoli Pasta on page 71 or Chicken
Pot Pie on page 25.

Chicago Style Pizza

MAKES 2-4 SERVINGS

2 tablespoons olive oil
1 store-bought pizza dough ball (1 pound)
8 ounces Italian sausage, uncooked
Kosher salt and fresh pepper to taste

1 1/2 cups mozzarella cheese, shredded
2/3 cup canned pasta or pizza sauce
1/4 cup Parmesan cheese, grated

1. Preheat the oven to 450°F, set the function to BAKE and timer to 10 minutes.

2. Pour the oil into a 9-inch round cake or pizza pan that has 2-inch sides.

3. Place the dough into the pan then flip over to coat both sides with oil.

4. Press and stretch the dough in the pan evenly until the sides are 1-inch tall.

5. Drop small bits of sausage all over dough, leaving a 3/4-inch border.

6. Sprinkle with salt, pepper and mozzarella.

7. Top with sauce then sprinkle with Parmesan.

8. Place the pan on the rack in the lower position then close the door.

9. Set the Vent Release Valve to SEAL, lower the Sealing Lever to the SEAL position and reset the timer.

10. Cook for 25-30 minutes or until well browned.

11. When cooking is complete, turn the Vent Release Valve to VENT and wait for all air to escape. Once vented, slowly raise the Sealing Lever and press the Door Release Button to open the door.

12. Remove pizza, garnish as desired and serve.

Chicken and Broccoli Pasta

MAKES 4 SERVINGS

1 can (10.75 ounces) cream of mushroom soup
2 cups chicken stock
3 cups leftover chicken or turkey, shredded
1 small yellow onion, chopped

8 ounces dry pasta
Kosher salt and fresh pepper to taste
1 bag (12 ounces) frozen broccoli
1 cup Parmesan cheese, grated

1. In a bowl whisk together the soup and stock then pour into the roasting pan.

2. Add remaining ingredients, except broccoli and Parmesan cheese then stir.

3. Cover tightly with aluminum foil then cut 4 small slits into the foil for steaming purposes.

4. Place the pan on the rack in the lower position then close the door.

5. Set the Vent Release Valve to SEAL, lower the Sealing Lever to the SEAL position and set the timer.

6. Set the oven to 350°F and function to BAKE.

7. Cook for 35 minutes.

8. When cooking is complete, turn the Vent Release Valve to VENT and wait for all air to escape. Once vented, slowly raise the Sealing Lever and press the Door Release Button to open the door.

9. Remove the pan, carefully remove the foil then scatter the broccoli and Parmesan cheese over the pan contents.

10. Return to oven uncovered then repeat step 5 and bake for an additional 15 minutes.

11. Garnish as desired and serve.

Baked Pierogies with Sour Cream

MAKES 4 SERVINGS

4 tablespoons unsalted butter
1 large yellow onion, sliced
Kosher salt and fresh pepper to taste
1 box (1 pound) frozen potato & cheese pierogies
Sour cream and chives, for serving

1. Preheat the oven to 450°F, set the function to BAKE and timer to 10 minutes.

2. Place the butter, onions, salt and pepper into the roasting pan.

3. Place the pan on the rack in the lower position then close the door.

4. Set the Vent Release Valve to SEAL, lower the Sealing Lever to the SEAL position and reset the timer.

5. Bake for 15 minutes or until butter and onions start to brown.

6. When cooking is complete, turn the Vent Release Valve to VENT and wait for all air to escape. Once vented, slowly raise the Sealing Lever and press the Door Release Button to open the door.

7. Remove the pan then quickly add the frozen pierogies evenly on top of the onions, flat-side up.

8. Cover tightly with aluminum foil and cut 4 small slits into the foil for steaming purposes; return to oven.

9. Repeat step 4 then cook for an additional 15 minutes or until pierogies are well steamed then remove foil and flip pierogies over using a spoon so that the pillowy side is facing up.

10. Continue to cook uncovered until they are beginning to brown and onions are deeply caramelized.

11. Remove, garnish as desired then serve with sour cream and chives.

Baked 1000 Island Pork Chops

MAKES 4 SERVINGS

4 large pork chops
Kosher salt and fresh pepper to taste
1/4 cup Parmesan cheese, grated
1/2 cup panko breadcrumbs
4 tablespoons 1000 Island dressing + more for serving

1. Preheat the oven to 450°F, set the function to BAKE and timer to 10 minutes.

2. Season pork chops on each side with salt and pepper then place on drip/baking pan.

3. Sprinkle the tops of the pork chops evenly with cheese and panko.

4. Place the pan on the rack in the middle position then close the door.

5. Set the Vent Release Valve to SEAL, lower the Sealing Lever to the SEAL position and reset the timer.

6. Bake for 10 minutes.

7. When cooking is complete, turn the Vent Release Valve to VENT and wait for all air to escape. Once vented, slowly raise the Sealing Lever and press the Door Release Button to open the door.

8. Remove pork chops, top the center of each chop with a tablespoon of 1000 Island dressing then return to oven.

9. Repeat step 5 then cook for an additional 8 minutes or until pork chops are brown and internal temperature registers 145°F on a meat thermometer.

10. Remove, garnish as desired and serve with additional 1000 Island dressing.

TIP

The brand I use in this recipe is an organic long grain rice from the big box stores. Because brands and sizes of rice vary greatly it is difficult to give exact cooking times. If your rice is still chewy, cover it again with the foil and let it stand for 5-10 minutes or cook for an additional 5 minutes.

Baked Brown Rice

MAKES 5-6 SERVINGS

2 cups brown rice
4 cups water
Kosher salt to taste (optional)
1 tablespoon olive oil

1. Line the roasting pan with heavy-duty aluminum foil then combine all ingredients in the pan and stir gently.

2. Cover pan tightly with aluminum foil then cut 4 small slits into the foil for steaming purposes.

3. Place the pan on the rack in the lower position then close the door.

4. Set the Vent Release Valve to SEAL, lower the Sealing Lever to the SEAL position and set the timer.

5. Set the oven to 450°F, function to BAKE.

6. Cook for 55 minutes.

7. When cooking is complete, turn the Vent Release Valve to VENT and wait for all air to escape. Once vented, slowly raise the Sealing Lever and press the Door Release Button to open the door.

8. Remove the pan, fluff the rice using a fork and serve.

Chocolate Mocha Cake

MAKES TWO 7-INCH ROUNDS

1/2 cup unsalted butter, softened
1 1/2 cups light brown sugar, packed
2 large eggs
2 teaspoons vanilla extract
1/2 cup good-quality cocoa powder
2 teaspoons baking soda
1 1/2 cups cake flour
2/3 cup sour cream
1 teaspoon instant coffee granules
2/3 cup water
Whipped cream, for layering and topping

1. Butter and flour two 7-inch round cake pans; set aside.

2. Place the butter and brown sugar into the bowl of a stand mixer fitted with the paddle.

3. Mix on medium speed for 5 minutes then scrape the bowl.

4. Add the eggs and vanilla then mix until combined; scrape the bowl again.

5. Add the cocoa, baking soda and cake flour then mix until blended; scrape the bowl.

6. Add remaining ingredients, except whipped cream, and mix until smooth.

7. Divide batter evenly between the two pans.

8. Preheat the oven to 350°F, set the function to BAKE and timer to 10 minutes.

9. Place the pans on the rack in the lower position then close the door.

10. Set the Vent Release Valve to SEAL, lower the Sealing Lever to the SEAL position and reset the timer.

11. Bake for 20-25 minutes or until a wooden pick inserted off-center comes out with just a few moist crumbs clinging to it.

12. When cooking is complete, turn the Vent Release Valve to VENT and wait for all air to escape. Once vented, slowly raise the Sealing Lever and press the Door Release Button to open the door.

13. Remove and let cool for 10 minutes before unmolding.

14. Let cool completely then split each layer horizontally using a long, thin knife to make 4 layers.

15. Frost and stack each layer with whipped cream then frost top and sides before serving.

TIP

To boost the coffee taste, stir 1-2 teaspoons instant coffee granules into the whipped cream before frosting the cake layers.

77

Chicken and Pesto Pizza

MAKES 2 SERVINGS

1 store-bought pizza dough ball (8 ounces)
All purpose flour, for the dough
2 tablespoons jarred pesto
1 cup mozzarella cheese, shredded
2 tablespoons Parmesan cheese, grated

1 cup leftover diced chicken or turkey
2 tablespoons sliced red onions
1/4 teaspoon chili flakes (optional)
Kosher salt and fresh pepper to taste
Fresh basil, for serving

1. Preheat the oven to 450°F, set the function to BAKE and timer to 10 minutes.

2. Stretch the dough into a rough rectangle or desired shape using flour to prevent sticking then place in the roasting pan or a pizza screen.

3. Brush or spoon the pesto over the dough then top with cheeses, chicken and onions.

4. Season with chili flakes, salt and pepper.

5. Place the pan on the rack in the middle position then close the door.

6. Set the Vent Release Valve to SEAL, lower the Sealing Lever to the SEAL position and reset the timer.

7. Cook for 7-10 minutes or until well browned and bubbly (turn pizza around halfway through the cooking cycle).

8. When cooking is complete, turn the Vent Release Valve to VENT and wait for all air to escape. Once vented, slowly raise the Sealing Lever and press the Door Release Button to open the door.

9. Remove pizza, top with basil, garnish as desired and serve.

Chicken Calzone

MAKES 2 SERVINGS

1 store-bought pizza dough ball (8 ounces)
All purpose flour, for the dough
1/4 cup jarred Alfredo or pasta sauce
1 garlic clove, minced
2 tablespoons olives
4 Provolone cheese slices

1 cup leftover chicken or turkey, shredded
1/2 bell pepper, sliced
Kosher salt and fresh pepper to taste
2 teaspoons olive oil
1 tablespoon Parmesan cheese, grated

1. Preheat the oven to 450°F, function to BAKE and timer to 10 minutes.

2. Stretch dough into a rough rectangle or desired shape using flour to prevent sticking then place dough in the roasting pan.

3. Spread the Alfredo sauce over half the dough then top with garlic, olives, Provolone, chicken and bell peppers. Season with salt and pepper.

4. Fold dough-only end over the dough half with the filling then push a fork around the edges to seal.

5. Brush top with oil, sprinkle with Parmesan then cut a small hole into the top crust to vent.

6. Place the pan on the rack in the lower position then close the door.

7. Set the Vent Release Valve to SEAL, lower the Sealing Lever to the SEAL position and reset the timer.

8. Cook for 20 minutes or until well browned and juices begin to bubble through the vent hole.

9. When cooking is complete, turn the Vent Release Valve to VENT and wait for all air to escape. Once vented, slowly raise the Sealing Lever and press the Door Release Button to open the door.

10. Remove calzone, garnish as desired and serve.

Italian Roast Turkey

MAKES 8 SERVINGS

2 pounds small red bliss potatoes
1 turkey (10 pounds), thawed
1 tablespoon olive oil
Kosher salt and fresh pepper to taste
2 lemons, halved
8 whole garlic cloves
A few rosemary sprigs
1 cup mixed olives
1/2 cup jarred pesto

1. Remove turkey from refrigerator. If desired, for a crispier skin and more even cooking, let the turkey rest at room temperature for 1 to 1 1/2 hours. Otherwise proceed to next step.

2. Preheat the oven to 450°F, set the function to ROAST and timer to 10 minutes.

3. Place the potatoes into the roasting pan.

4. Tie the turkey according to trussing instructions on page 5 then place on top of potatoes in the pan.

5. Drizzle turkey with oil then season with salt and pepper.

6. Place 1 lemon half, a few garlic cloves and a rosemary sprig into turkey cavity.

7. Scatter remaining ingredients, except pesto, around the turkey.

8. Place the pan on the rack in the lower position then close the door.

9. Set the Vent Release Valve to SEAL, lower the Sealing Lever to the SEAL position and reset the timer.

10. Roast turkey for 55 minutes or until well browned and juices are boiling.

11. When cooking is complete, turn the Vent Release Valve to VENT and wait for all air to escape. Once vented, slowly raise the Sealing Lever and press the Door Release Button to open the door.

12. Internal temperature of turkey should register 165°F on a meat thermometer. If more cooking is needed, repeat step 9 and cook for an additional 5-10 minutes or until internal temperature reaches 165°F.

13. Allow turkey to rest for 15 minutes before carving.

14. While turkey is resting, spoon 1 cup of the juices from around the turkey into a small pan then stir in the pesto.

15. Serve turkey and vegetables with pesto sauce.

TIP

The pressure oven's ability to cook this turkey in under one hour combined with this non-traditional recipe makes it possible to enjoy turkey anytime and not just for Thanksgiving.

Easiest Raspberry Soufflés with Raspberry Puree

MAKES 6 SERVINGS

1 bag (12 ounces) frozen raspberries, thawed
Unsalted butter and sugar, for prepping ramekins
5 large egg whites
1/4 teaspoon cream of tartar
2/3 cup granulated sugar
1 tablespoon cornstarch
Powdered sugar, for dusting

TIP

Keep all tools needed for the egg whites grease-free. This will allow you to achieve perfect meringue with the ability to nicely lift the soufflés above the rims of the ramekins.

1. Place raspberries into a blender and puree until fairly smooth; set aside.

2. Butter 6 straight-sided ramekins, sprinkle with sugar then place on a baking sheet.

3. Using a hand mixer or stand mixer fitted with the whisk attachment, mix the egg whites in a bowl until foamy.

4. Add the cream of tartar and sugar then beat on medium-high speed for 3-4 minutes or until soft peaks form and tips curl over.

5. Place 1/2 cup of the raspberry puree into a separate bowl then whisk in the cornstarch; reserve remaining raspberry puree for serving.

6. Pour the raspberry mixture over the egg whites and fold in gently until combined.

7. Divide mixture between ramekins, filling each until slightly mounded.

8. Preheat the oven to 400°F, set the function to BAKE and timer to 10 minutes.

9. Place the pan on the rack in the lower position then close the door.

10. Set the Vent Release Valve to SEAL, lower the Sealing Lever to the SEAL position and reset the timer.

11. Bake for 7-10 minutes or until well-risen and brown on top.

12. When cooking is complete, turn the Vent Release Valve to VENT and wait for all air to escape. Once vented, slowly raise the Sealing Lever and press the Door Release Button to open the door.

13. Remove carefully, dust with powdered sugar and serve with reserved raspberry puree.

One-Bowl Cupcakes

MAKES 12-18 SERVINGS

1 cup unsalted butter, very soft
2 1/3 cups granulated sugar
5 large eggs
1 cup whole milk
1 cup sour cream

1 tablespoon vanilla extract
3 cups cake flour
3/4 teaspoon baking soda
2 1/4 teaspoons baking powder
2 teaspoons kosher salt

1. Preheat the oven to 350°F, set the function to BAKE and timer to 10 minutes.

2. Line a cupcake pan with paper liners; set aside.

3. Using a hand mixer, cream the butter and sugar in a mixing bowl until fluffy.

4. Scrape the bowl then add the eggs, milk, sour cream and vanilla; blend for 20 seconds.

5. Mix in remaining ingredients until just blended then fill liners 2/3 full.

6. Place the pan on the rack in the lower position then close the door.

7. Set the Vent Release Valve to SEAL, lower the Sealing Lever to the SEAL position and reset the timer.

8. Bake for 20-25 minutes or until golden brown.

9. When cooking is complete, turn the Vent Release Valve to VENT and wait for all air to escape. Once vented, slowly raise the Sealing Lever and press the Door Release Button to open the door.

10. Remove and let cool completely. Repeat with remaining batter.

11. Frost or pipe cupcakes with the Meringue on page 33 and serve.

Oven Beef Stew

MAKES 3-4 SERVINGS

1 pound beef chuck, cut into 1-inch cubes
2 tablespoons bottled soy sauce
1 tablespoon jarred beef bouillon base or to taste
2 tablespoons cornstarch or flour
Fresh pepper to taste
3 cups beef stock

1/4 cup ketchup
1 tablespoon bottled Worcestershire sauce
1 bay leaf
1 medium yellow onion, chunked
1 Russet potato, chunked
1 carrot, chunked

1. Place beef, soy sauce, bouillon, cornstarch and pepper into the roasting pan.

2. Mix by hand (use gloves if desired) until the beef is thoroughly coated then add remaining ingredients to the pan. Cover tightly with aluminum foil then cut 4 small slits into the foil for steaming purposes.

3. Place the pan on the rack in the lower position then close the door.

4. Set the Vent Release Valve to SEAL, lower the Sealing Lever to the SEAL position and set the timer.

5. Set the oven to 325°F and function to BAKE.

6. Cook for 80 minutes.

7. When cooking is complete, turn the Vent Release Valve to VENT and wait for all air to escape. Once vented, slowly raise the Sealing Lever and press the Door Release Button to open the door.

8. Remove pan, discard the foil and test meat, it should be fall-apart tender.

9. Discard bay leaf, garnish as desired and serve.

New York Style Browned Cheesecake

MAKES 8 SERVINGS

For the Crust:
12 graham crackers
3 tablespoons light brown sugar, packed
4 tablespoons unsalted butter, melted

For the Filling:
4 packages (8 ounces each) cream cheese, softened
1 cup sugar
1/4 cup sour cream
6 large eggs

1. Combine all crust ingredients in a food processor and pulse until combined. Press mixture into the bottom of an 8-inch springform pan; set aside.

2. Rinse food processor bowl then add all filling ingredients and process until smooth. Pour mixture into the crust in the springform pan.

3. Place the pan on the rack in the lower position then close the door.

4. Set the Vent Release Valve to SEAL, lower the Sealing Lever to the SEAL position and set the timer.

5. Set the oven to 350°F and function to BAKE.

6. Cook for 50 minutes or until well browned, puffed and cracked in places.

7. When cooking is complete, turn the Vent Release Valve to VENT and wait for all air to escape. Once vented, slowly raise the Sealing Lever and press the Door Release Button to open the door.

8. Remove cake, garnish as desired and serve hot.

No Meat One Pot Pasta

MAKES 4 SERVINGS

1 cup ricotta cheese + more for serving
1 large yellow onion, chopped
1 small sweet potato, cubed
2 cups kale leaves, torn
8 ounces dry pasta
2 cups vegetable stock

1/2 cup olives
1 teaspoon dried sage
Kosher salt and fresh pepper to taste
1/4 cup grated Parmesan cheese, for serving
Balsamic glaze, store-bought, for serving

1. Combine all ingredients, except Parmesan cheese and balsamic glaze in the roasting pan.

2. Cover tightly with aluminum foil then cut 4 small slits into the foil for steaming purposes.

3. Place the pan on the rack in the lower position then close the door.

4. Set the Vent Release Valve to SEAL, lower the Sealing Lever to the SEAL position and set the timer.

5. Set the oven to 350°F and function to BAKE.

6. Cook for 45 minutes.

7. When cooking is complete, turn the Vent Release Valve to VENT and wait for all air to escape. Once vented, slowly raise the Sealing Lever and press the Door Release Button to open the door.

8. Remove pan, garnish as desired and serve with Parmesan cheese and balsamic glaze.

Hash Brown Casserole

MAKES 4-6 SERVINGS

1 small yellow onion, chopped
2 pounds frozen hash browns, micro-thawed
1/4 cup unsalted butter
1 can (11.75 ounces) cream of chicken soup

1 cup sour cream
1 cup mild Cheddar cheese, grated
Maple syrup, for serving (optional)

1. In a bowl, mix together all ingredients, except syrup, then spoon into a greased roasting pan.

2. Place the pan on the rack in the lower position then close the door.

3. Set the Vent Release Valve to SEAL, lower the Sealing Lever to the SEAL position and set the timer.

4. Set the oven to 350°F and function to BAKE.

5. Cook for 35 minutes.

6. When cooking is complete, turn the Vent Release Valve to VENT and wait for all air to escape. Once vented, slowly raise the Sealing Lever and press the Door Release Button to open the door.

7. Remove casserole, garnish as desired and serve with maple syrup if desired.

Holiday Baked Brie

MAKES 6-10 SERVINGS

1 package (14.1 ounces) refrigerated pie crusts
2 large eggs, well beaten
1 wheel Brie cheese (16 ounces) with rind on
1/4 cup jam or preserves such as raspberry
1 tablespoon granulated sugar

1. Unroll both pie crusts from the package then place one on your counter and the other on the parchment-lined drip/baking pan.

2. Use desired 2-inch cookie cutters and make cut-outs from the pie crust on the counter.

3. Brush cut-outs and whole pie crust on pan with beaten egg.

4. Place whole Brie on whole pie crust then spoon jam into center.

5. Gather up the edges then bring them up, pressing them inward up to the jam.

6. Place cut-outs around jam opening, egg-side down.

7. Brush entire pie crust and cut-outs with beaten egg then sprinkle with sugar.

8. Place the pan on the rack in the lower position then close the door.

9. Set the oven to 375°F and function to BAKE.

10. Bake for 35 minutes or until crust is golden brown.

11. When baking is complete, remove from oven and serve warm.

Cinnamon Rolls with Cream Cheese Icing

MAKES 9 SERVINGS

For the Buns:
1 store-bought pizza dough ball (1 pound)

For the Filling:
4 tablespoons unsalted butter, melted
2 teaspoons vanilla extract
1 cup brown sugar
1 tablespoon ground cinnamon

For the Cream Cheese Icing:
1 cup powdered sugar
1 package (8 ounces) cream cheese, softened

1. Roll out the pizza dough into a large rectangle.

2. Stir all filling ingredients together using a spatula.

3. Spread the filling over the dough then roll up the dough. Pinch the seams to seal then cut into 9 rolls.

4. Apply nonstick cooking spray to the roasting pan.

5. Place the rolls into the pan then cover and let rise in the refrigerator for a minimum of 1 hour or overnight.

6. Place the pan on the rack in the lower position then close the door.

7. Set the Vent Release Valve to SEAL, lower the Sealing Lever to the SEAL position and set the timer.

8. Set the oven to 350°F and function to BAKE.

9. Cook for 35 minutes or until well risen and brown.

10. While rolls are baking, stir together the cream cheese icing ingredients.

11. When cooking is complete, turn the Vent Release Valve to VENT and wait for all air to escape. Once vented, slowly raise the Sealing Lever and press the Door Release Button to open the door.

12. Remove rolls, top with cream cheese icing and serve warm.

TIP

This is a great dish to prepare in advance. Follow the recipe until step 5 then wrap and freeze for up to 1 month. You can thaw overnight before continuing to bake per recipe instructions.

Honey Garlic Pork Chops

MAKES 4 SERVINGS

4 large pork chops
Kosher salt and fresh pepper to taste
1 tablespoon unsalted butter, softened
2 teaspoons spicy mustard
2 garlic cloves, minced
1 green onion, minced
2 tablespoons honey

1. Season both sides of the pork chops with salt and pepper then place on the drip/baking pan.

2. In a small bowl whisk together remaining ingredients then brush on both sides of the pork chops.

3. Place the pan on the rack in the middle position then close the door.

4. Set the Vent Release Valve to SEAL, lower the Sealing Lever to the SEAL position and set the timer.

5. Set the oven to 450°F and function to BAKE.

6. Cook for 15 minutes or until honey mixture is bubbly, pork chops are brown around the edges and internal temperature reaches 145°F on a meat thermometer.

7. When cooking is complete, turn the Vent Release Valve to VENT and wait for all air to escape. Once vented, slowly raise the Sealing Lever and press the Door Release Button to open the door.

8. Remove chops, garnish as desired and serve.

For a lower fat alternative, try using chicken sausages or even a vegetarian version. The pressure oven will make any type of sausage moist and juicy.

Italian Sausage and Peppers

MAKES 6 SERVINGS

6 Italian sausages links, uncooked
1 large yellow onion, sliced
2 bell peppers, sliced
A few rosemary sprigs
1 tablespoon olive oil
Kosher salt and fresh pepper to taste

1. Place sausages, onions, peppers and rosemary on the drip/baking pan then drizzle with oil. Season with salt and pepper.

2. Place the pan on the rack in the lower position then close the door.

3. Set the Vent Release Valve to SEAL, lower the Sealing Lever to the SEAL position and set the timer.

4. Set the oven to 450°F and function to ROAST.

5. Cook for 35 minutes or until well browned and vegetables are tender.

6. When cooking is complete, turn the Vent Release Valve to VENT and wait for all air to escape. Once vented, slowly raise the Sealing Lever and press the Door Release Button to open the door.

7. Remove pan, slice sausages into rounds, toss with the vegetables then garnish as desired and serve.

For firmer and brighter vegetables, add them during the last 30 minutes of cooking.

Corned Beef and Cabbage

MAKES 3-4 SERVINGS

3-4 pounds corned beef, flat cut
2 cups water
1/4 small head cabbage, wedged
8 small red potatoes
2 carrots, sliced

1. Place all ingredients into the roasting pan (add the spice packet that often comes with the corned beef if included).

2. Cover tightly with aluminum foil then cut 4 small slits into the foil for steaming purposes.

3. Place the pan on the rack in the lower position then close the door.

4. Set the Vent Release Valve to SEAL, lower the Sealing Lever to the SEAL position and set the timer.

5. Set the oven to 375°F and function to ROAST.

6. Cook for 4 hours or until meat is fall-apart tender.

7. When cooking is complete, turn the Vent Release Valve to VENT and wait for all air to escape. Once vented, slowly raise the Sealing Lever and press the Door Release Button to open the door.

8. Remove pan, skim off excess fat then serve either sliced or pulled into chunks.

<blockquote>
TIP

You can substitute sweet potatoes for the Russet potatoes. You might need to adjust the cooking time slightly as sweet potatoes tend to get dark quicker.
</blockquote>

Crispy Oven Fries

MAKES 2-4 SERVINGS

2 large Russet potatoes
1 tablespoon canola oil
Kosher salt to taste

1. Preheat the oven to 450°F, set the function to BAKE and timer to 10 minutes.

2. Slice either peeled or unpeeled potatoes into long, thin sticks.

3. Rinse potato sticks under cold water then dry thoroughly using a towel.

4. Transfer potato sticks to a large bowl then add remaining ingredients and toss to coat.

5. Pour bowl contents out onto the drip/baking pan then spread into an even layer. Do not let the potatoes touch or be more than one layer deep.

6. Place the pan on the rack in the lower position then close the door.

7. Set the Vent Release Valve to SEAL, lower the Sealing Lever to the SEAL position and reset the timer.

8. Cook 20-25 minutes or until golden brown and crispy.

9. When cooking is complete, turn the Vent Release Valve to VENT and wait for all air to escape. Once vented, slowly raise the Sealing Lever and press the Door Release Button to open the door.

10. Remove fries, garnish as desired and serve.

Leg of Lamb with Mint Sauce

MAKES 4-5 SERVINGS

For the Lamb:
Boneless leg of lamb roast (3 pounds)
12 whole garlic cloves
12 short rosemary sprigs
2 tablespoons olive oil, divided
Kosher salt and fresh pepper to taste
1 pound fingerling or other small potatoes

For the Mint Sauce:
1 bunch fresh mint, leaves only
2 tablespoons apple cider vinegar
2 teaspoons dry mustard powder
1 garlic clove, chopped
1/4 cup granulated sugar
2/3 cup mayonnaise

1. Using a paring knife, cut random slits into the roast then insert a whole garlic clove and a rosemary sprig into each slit, pushing it in with your finger. Drizzle with some oil then season with salt and pepper.

2. Place potatoes into the roasting pan then season with remaining oil, salt and pepper. Place the roast on top of the potatoes.

3. Place the pan on the rack in the lower position then close the door.

4. Set the Vent Release Valve to SEAL, lower the Sealing Lever to the SEAL position and set the timer.

5. Set the oven to 450°F and function to ROAST.

6. Cook for 60 minutes or until desired doneness is achieved, 115°F for a rosy center, 135°F for well-done. Use a meat thermometer to monitor temperature.

7. While the roast is cooking, combine all mint sauce ingredients in a blender. Add some salt and pepper then blend until mint leaves are small flecks; set aside.

8. When cooking is complete, turn the Vent Release Valve to VENT and wait for all air to escape. Once vented, slowly raise the Sealing Lever and press the Door Release Button to open the door.

9. Remove lamb and let stand for 10 minutes before carving. Garnish as desired and serve with mint sauce.

Loaded Chicken Nachos

MAKES 4-5 SERVINGS

2 cups leftover turkey or chicken, diced
1/2 cup Ranch dressing
1 bag (10 ounces) tortilla chips or as needed
1 1/2 cups mixed Mexican-style cheese, shredded
1 large tomato, diced

1 large jalapeño pepper, diced
1/2 cup black olives, sliced
Sour cream, for serving
Chopped cilantro, for serving

1. Preheat the oven to 400°F, set the function to ROAST and timer to 10 minutes (you will not be using pressure for this recipe).

2. In a bowl, stir together the chicken and ranch dressing.

3. Place half of the tortilla chips on the drip/baking pan then top with half of the chicken, cheese, tomatoes, jalapeño and olives. Repeat to make a second layer.

4. Place the pan on the rack in the lower position then close the door and reset timer.

5. Roast for 15-20 minutes or until cheese is melted and chips are brown along the edges.

6. When cooking is complete, remove nachos and serve hot with sour cream and cilantro.

Spatchcock Chicken

MAKES 4 SERVINGS

4 tablespoons unsalted butter, softened
1 tablespoon jarred chicken bouillon base or to taste
1/2 teaspoon paprika
1 teaspoon onion powder
1 teaspoon poultry seasoning
Kosher salt and fresh pepper to taste
1 whole chicken (4 pounds)

1. In a small mixing bowl, stir together the butter, bouillon, paprika, onion powder, poultry seasoning, salt and pepper.

2. Using sturdy scissors (and gloves if you prefer), cut down either side of the backbone and completely remove it, you can use either side of the tail as a guide for where to start snipping or ask your butcher to do this for you.

3. Turn chicken over, breast-side up, and press down firmly on the breast to flatten it. Using your fingers, smear half of the butter mixture all over chicken then slip the other half under the skin to flavor the meat.

4. Place chicken into the roasting pan.

5. Place the pan on the rack in the lower position then close the door.

6. Set the Vent Release Valve to SEAL, lower the Sealing Lever to the SEAL position and set the timer.

7. Set the oven to 450°F and function to ROAST.

8. Cook for 35 minutes.

9. When cooking is complete, turn the Vent Release Valve to VENT and wait for all air to escape. Once vented, slowly raise the Sealing Lever and press the Door Release Button to open the door.

10. Remove chicken and baste with the pan juices.

11. Return chicken to oven and cook for an additional 10 minutes or until brown and the thigh registers 165°F on a meat thermometer.

12. Remove, let rest for 5 minutes then carve and serve with the flavorful juices in the pan.

TIP

Make this recipe stretch up to 4 meals! Leftovers are great in the Chicken Pot Pie on page 25, the Chicken Pesto Pasta on page 40, the Chicken Calzone on page 79 or the Buffalo Chicken Dip on page 62.

TIP

You can make this recipe using pumpkin, Hubbard, kabocha or acorn squash as well as the butternut variety.

Maple Roasted Butternut Squash

MAKES 4 SERVINGS

1 butternut squash, halved and seeded
2 tablespoons unsalted butter, melted
2 tablespoons maple syrup + more for drizzling
2 tablespoons dried cranberries
2 tablespoons pine nuts
2 tablespoons feta cheese, crumbled
1 cup fresh kale, chopped
2 tablespoons parsley, chopped
Kosher salt and fresh pepper to taste

1. Place squash halves on the drip/baking pan.

2. In a medium mixing bowl, combine remaining ingredients then divide between the hollows in the squash. Season the neck of each squash with additional maple syrup, salt and pepper.

3. Place the pan on the rack in the lower position then close the door.

4. Set the Vent Release Valve to SEAL, lower the Sealing Lever to the SEAL position and set the timer.

5. Set the oven to 450°F and function to BAKE.

6. Cook for 45 minutes or until squash is tender and filling is well browned.

7. When cooking is complete, turn the Vent Release Valve to VENT and wait for all air to escape. Once vented, slowly raise the Sealing Lever and press the Door Release Button to open the door.

8. Remove squash, garnish as desired and serve.

Mom's Apple Pie

MAKES 8-10 SERVINGS

6 large Granny Smith apples, peeled and sliced
2/3 cup granulated sugar + more for topping
2 tablespoons all purpose flour

2 teaspoons ground cinnamon
1 package (14.1 ounces) refrigerated pie crusts
1 tablespoon unsalted butter, cold

1. In a large bowl, toss together the apple slices, sugar, flour and cinnamon.

2. Unroll one of the pie crusts from the package onto a greased 9-inch pie pan then top with the apples. Dot the top with little pinches of butter then add the top crust.

3. Crimp edges together by pressing all around using a fork. Cut a steam vent hole into the top.

4. Brush the top of the pie crust with a little water then sprinkle with additional sugar.

5. Place pie on the drip/baking pan then place on the rack in the lower position then close the door.

6. Set the Vent Release Valve to SEAL, lower the Sealing Lever to the SEAL position and set the timer.

7. Set the oven to 450°F and function to BAKE.

8. Cook for 45 minutes or until well browned and juices are bubbling through the vent hole.

9. When cooking is complete, turn the Vent Release Valve to VENT and wait for all air to escape. Once vented, slowly raise the Sealing Lever and press the Door Release Button to open the door.

10. Remove pie, garnish as desired and serve slightly warm.

Oven BBQ Chicken

MAKES 4-6 SERVINGS

4-6 pieces fresh chicken (all breasts if you like, skin on or off)
1 cup bottled BBQ sauce
2 tablespoons BBQ seasoning

1. Places chicken pieces into the roasting pan.

2. Liberally brush BBQ sauce over chicken then season with BBQ seasoning.

3. Place the pan on the rack in the lower position then close the door.

4. Set the Vent Release Valve to SEAL, lower the Sealing Lever to the SEAL position and set the timer.

5. Set the oven to 450°F and function to BAKE.

6. Cook for 25 minutes or until internal temperature reaches 165°F on a meat thermometer (if chicken is getting dark too quickly, loosely cover with aluminum foil).

7. When cooking is complete, turn the Vent Release Valve to VENT and wait for all air to escape. Once vented, slowly raise the Sealing Lever and press the Door Release Button to open the door.

8. Remove chicken, garnish as desired and serve.

TIP

If you prefer only the white meat of the chicken, especially boneless, skinless chicken breasts, ensure that you do not over cook them. They are very lean and can dry out quickly. Cook just until internal temperature reaches 165°F on a meat thermometer. Do not cook any longer to achieve the juiciest and thoroughly cooked chicken.

TIP

The timing for this recipe is written for basmati rice, which is long and thin in shape. Add 5 minutes cooking time if using a long-grain white rice or 10 minutes for short-grain white rice.

Oven Steamed Rice

MAKES 4-6 SERVINGS

2 cups white basmati rice
3 1/2 cups water
1 tablespoon olive oil
Kosher salt to taste (optional)

1. Line the roasting pan with heavy duty aluminum foil then pour all ingredients into the pan and stir gently (you do not need to rinse oven rice).

2. Cover tightly with aluminum foil then cut 4 small slits into the foil for steaming purposes.

3. Place the pan on the rack in the lower position then close the door.

4. Set the Vent Release Valve to SEAL, lower the Sealing Lever to the SEAL position and set the timer.

5. Set the oven to 450°F and function to BAKE.

6. Cook for 25 minutes.

7. When cooking is complete, turn the Vent Release Valve to VENT and wait for all air to escape. Once vented, slowly raise the Sealing Lever and press the Door Release Button to open the door.

8. Remove rice, garnish as desired and serve.

┌──────── TIP ────────┐
This recipe is great using
pork chops, fish, steak or
even lamb chops instead
of chicken.

Parmesan Crispy Chicken Breasts

MAKES 4 SERVINGS

4 chicken breasts
Kosher salt and fresh pepper to taste
1/4 teaspoon paprika
2 teaspoons onion powder

1/4 cup mayonnaise or Greek yogurt
1/3 cup Parmesan cheese, grated
1/4 cup panko breadcrumbs

1. Preheat the oven to 450°F, set the function to BAKE and timer to 10 minutes.

2. Lightly season both sides of the chicken with salt and pepper then place on drip/baking pan.

3. In a bowl, mix together the paprika, onion powder and mayonnaise then smear onto tops of chicken.

4. Stir together remaining ingredients then evenly top each breast with this mixture.

5. Place the pan on the rack in the lower position then close the door.

6. Set the Vent Release Valve to SEAL, lower the Sealing Lever to the SEAL position and reset the timer.

7. Cook for 18 minutes or until well browned and chicken registers 165°F on a meat thermometer.

8. When cooking is complete, turn the Vent Release Valve to VENT and wait for all air to escape. Once vented, slowly raise the Sealing Lever and press the Door Release Button to open the door.

9. Remove chicken, garnish as desired and serve.

Pineapple Upside Down Cake

MAKES 10-12 SERVINGS

For the Base:
4 tablespoons unsalted butter, softened
6 tablespoons light brown sugar
10 fresh pineapple slices, 1/2-inch thick, cored
10 cherries, fresh or the maraschino variety

For the Cake:
1 1/3 cups granulated sugar
1/2 cup unsalted butter, softened
2 large eggs
1 1/3 cups pineapple juice
1 tablespoon vanilla extract
4 teaspoons baking powder
2 2/3 cups all purpose flour

TIP

For a gluten-free version of this cake, substitute
2 2/3 cups gluten-free flour mix for the all
purpose flour called for in the recipe. No other
changes are needed.

1. Spread butter on the bottom and sides of a 10-inch round cake pan.

2. Sprinkle buttered pan with brown sugar and twirl to coat all of the butter evenly.

3. Press pineapple slices and cherries evenly into the butter in the bottom of the pan.

4. In a mixing bowl, combine all cake ingredients in the order listed using a whisk until batter is smooth. Pour over pineapple-lined pan and smooth the top.

5. Place the pan on the rack in the lower position then close the door.

6. Set the Vent Release Valve to SEAL, lower the Sealing Lever to the SEAL position and set the timer.

7. Set the oven to 350°F and function to BAKE.

8. Cook for 40 minutes or until well browned and a wooden pick inserted off-center comes out clean.

9. When cooking is complete, turn the Vent Release Valve to VENT and wait for all air to escape. Once vented, slowly raise the Sealing Lever and press the Door Release Button to open the door.

10. Remove cake, let cool for 10 minutes then carefully loosen the edges using a table knife and invert onto a rimmed serving plate.

Peach Pie a la Mode

MAKES 8 SERVINGS

8 large ripe peaches, pitted and sliced
1/2 cup granulated sugar or to taste
3 tablespoons all purpose flour
1/8 teaspoon ground cinnamon

2 teaspoons lemon juice
1 package (14.1 ounces) refrigerated pie crusts
1 tablespoon unsalted butter, cold
Ice cream, for serving

1. In a large bowl, toss together the peaches, sugar, flour, cinnamon and lemon juice.

2. Unroll one of the pie crusts from the package onto a greased 9-inch pie pan then add the bowl contents.

3. Dot the top with little pinches of the butter then add the top crust and crimp the pie edges together using a fork.

4. Brush the top of the pie crust with a little water then sprinkle with additional sugar and cut a steam vent hole into the top crust.

5. Place pan on the rack in the lower position then close the door.

6. Set the Vent Release Valve to SEAL, lower the Sealing Lever to the SEAL position and set the timer.

7. Set the oven to 450°F and function to BAKE.

8. Cook for 45 minutes or until well browned and juices are bubbling through the vent hole.

9. When cooking is complete, turn the Vent Release Valve to VENT and wait for all air to escape. Once vented, slowly raise the Sealing Lever and press the Door Release Button to open the door.

10. Remove pie, garnish as desired and serve slightly warm with ice cream.

TIP

This is great served over the Oven Steamed Rice on page 104.

Pizza Style Chicken Breasts

MAKES 4 SERVINGS

4 boneless, skinless chicken breasts
Kosher salt and fresh pepper to taste
1 jar (24 ounces) pasta sauce
1 small can (3 ounces) sliced black olives, drained
1/2 cup bell peppers, chopped

1 small yellow onion, chopped
16 pepperoni slices, cut into small strips
1/4 cup Parmesan cheese, grated
1 cup mozzarella cheese, shredded

1. Place chicken into the roasting pan then season with salt and pepper.

2. Pour pasta sauce over the chicken then top with remaining ingredients.

3. Place the pan on the rack in the lower position then close the door.

4. Set the Vent Release Valve to SEAL, lower the Sealing Lever to the SEAL position and set the timer.

5. Set the oven to 450°F and function to BAKE.

6. Cook for 35 minutes or until brown and bubbly and internal temperature of chicken reaches 165°F on a meat thermometer.

7. When cooking is complete, turn the Vent Release Valve to VENT and wait for all air to escape. Once vented, slowly raise the Sealing Lever and press the Door Release Button to open the door.

8. Remove chicken, garnish as desired and serve.

Savory Corn Casserole

MAKES 8 SERVINGS

1 can (14.75 ounces) corn
3 green onions, sliced
6 eggs, beaten
2 sleeves saltine crackers, crumbled
1 cup Parmesan cheese, grated
2 cups half & half
3 tablespoons granulated sugar
2 teaspoons kosher salt
Fresh pepper to taste

1. In a large mixing bowl, combine all ingredients. Mix well then pour into the greased roasting pan.

2. Place the pan on the rack in the lower position then close the door.

3. Set the Vent Release Valve to SEAL, lower the Sealing Lever to the SEAL position and set the timer.

4. Set the oven to 350°F and function to BAKE.

5. Bake for 45 minutes or until well browned and a knife inserted in the center comes out clean.

6. When cooking is complete, turn the Vent Release Valve to VENT and wait for all air to escape. Once vented, slowly raise the Sealing Lever and press the Door Release Button to open the door.

7. Remove casserole, garnish as desired and serve.

TIP
Seven-grain blend is made up of wheat berries, rye flakes, rolled oats, sunflower seeds, flax seed, poppy seeds and millet that you combine yourself.

Seven Grain Rolls

MAKES 12 ROLLS

1 1/3 cups water, room temperature
2 tablespoons olive oil
1 large egg
2 tablespoons powdered milk
1 teaspoon apple cider vinegar

1 tablespoon kosher salt
1 tablespoon granulated sugar
1 cup seven-grain blend + more for rolling
3 cups unbleached bread flour + more for rolling
1 envelope (1 tablespoon) rapid rise yeast

1. Combine all ingredients in the bowl of a stand mixer fitted with the dough hook. Mix on low speed for 10 minutes then remove and let rest for 1 hour.

2. Cut dough into 12 equal pieces then roll each into a ball using more flour if sticky. Dip each ball in more seven-grain blend then place seam-side down into a greased roasting pan. Refrigerate rolls at this point for up to 24 hours before baking if desired.

3. Cover and let rise for 45 minutes or until doubled in size then place the pan on the rack in the lower position and close the door.

4. Set the Vent Release Valve to SEAL, lower the Sealing Lever to the SEAL position and set the timer.

5. Set the oven to 350°F and function to BAKE.

6. Bake for 20-25 minutes or until well risen and brown.

7. When cooking is complete, turn the Vent Release Valve to VENT and wait for all air to escape. Once vented, slowly raise the Sealing Lever and press the Door Release Button to open the door.

8. Remove rolls and serve.

┌─────── TIP ───────┐
These potatoes are great
served with the Bacon
Wrapped Meatloaf on
page 44.
└───────────────────┘

Scalloped Potatoes

MAKES 4 SERVINGS

1/2 of a small yellow onion, chopped
Kosher salt and fresh pepper to taste
3 tablespoons all purpose flour or cornstarch
2 tablespoons unsalted butter, melted
1 tablespoon jarred chicken or vegetable bouillon base or to taste
2 cups whole milk
1/4 cup heavy cream
4 large Russet potatoes, thinly sliced

1. In a bowl, whisk together all ingredients, except potatoes.

2. Place potatoes into the roasting pan then pour milk mixture evenly over the potatoes.

3. Place the pan on the rack in the lower position then close the door.

4. Set the Vent Release Valve to SEAL, lower the Sealing Lever to the SEAL position and set the timer.

5. Set the oven to 450°F and function to BAKE.

6. Cook for 50 minutes or until brown and bubbly. Potatoes should be soft when pierced with a knife.

7. When cooking is complete, turn the Vent Release Valve to VENT and wait for all air to escape. Once vented, slowly raise the Sealing Lever and press the Door Release Button to open the door.

8. Remove potatoes, garnish as desired and serve hot.

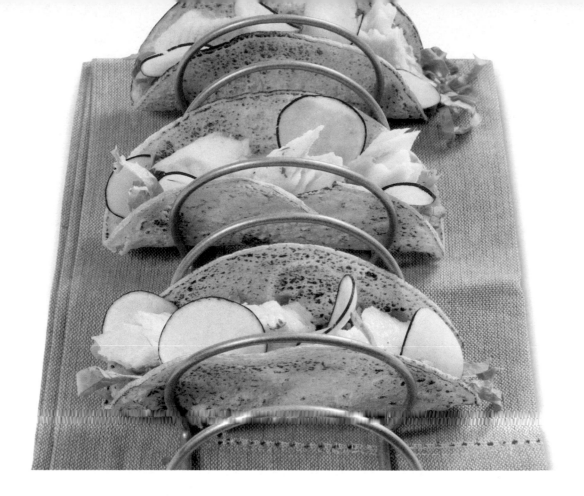

Fish Tacos

MAKES 4 SERVINGS

4 tilapia fillets or other mild white fish
2 tablespoons olive oil
2 garlic cloves, minced
Zest and juice of 1/2 lime

2 teaspoons chipotle chile powder, or to taste
Kosher salt to taste
Tortillas, lettuce and radishes, for serving
8 cilantro sprigs, chopped

1. Preheat the oven to 450°F, set the function to BROIL and timer to 10 minutes.

2. Fit drip/baking pan with the broil rack insert, apply nonstick cooking spray to it then place fish on the rack.

3. In a small bowl whisk together the oil, garlic, lime, chipotle and salt.

4. Spread mixture on both sides of each fish fillet.

5. Place the pan on the rack in the upper position then close the door.

6. Set the Vent Release Valve to SEAL, lower the Sealing Lever to the SEAL position and reset the timer.

7. Broil for 6-8 minutes or until fish is opaque.

8. When cooking is complete, turn the Vent Release Valve to VENT and wait for all air to escape. Once vented, slowly raise the Sealing Lever and press the Door Release Button to open the door.

9. Remove pan, gently flake the fish and serve with tortillas, lettuce, radishes and cilantro.

Proposal or Engagement Roast Chicken

MAKES 4-6 SERVINGS

4 tablespoons unsalted butter, softened
2 garlic cloves, minced
1/2 teaspoon fresh rosemary, chopped
1/2 teaspoon fresh thyme
1 tablespoon jarred chicken bouillon base or to taste
Kosher salt and fresh pepper to taste
1 whole chicken (about 4 pounds), tied
1 fresh lemon, halved

1. Preheat the oven to 450°F, set the function to ROAST and timer to 10 minutes.

2. In a mixing bowl, stir together the butter, garlic, rosemary, thyme, bouillon, salt and pepper.

3. Pat chicken dry then use your fingers to gently separate the skin from around the breast and top of thighs (do not remove the skin, just create a space to add the butter mixture). Gently pick up a small dollop of butter mixture and smear it over the breast between the skin and flesh. Smear additional butter mixture over the other side of the breast and the tops of each thigh. Smear remaining butter mixture over the exterior of the whole chicken then squeeze lemon all over and season with additional pepper.

4. Place the chicken in the roasting pan.

5. Place the pan on the rack in the lower position then close the door.

6. Set the Vent Release Valve to SEAL, lower the Sealing Lever to the SEAL position and reset the timer.

7. Cook for 35 minutes then turn the Vent Release Valve to VENT and wait for all air to escape. Once vented, slowly raise the Sealing Lever and press the Door Release Button to open the door.

8. Remove chicken, baste with the juices in the pan, return to oven, repeat step 6 and cook for an additional 10 minutes or until well browned and thickest part of thigh registers 165°F on a meat thermometer.

9. Remove, let stand for 10 minutes, then garnish as desired and serve.

TIP

To make this a complete meal, simply add potatoes, onions and carrots to the roasting pan before cooking.

German Pot Roast

MAKES 4 SERVINGS

1 beef chuck roast (3-4 pounds)
Kosher salt and fresh pepper to taste
1 cup beef stock
1 bay leaf
2 garlic cloves, minced
1/2 cup Kosher dill pickle, diced
1 large white onion, chopped

1/2 cup grainy mustard
2 tablespoons brown sugar
1/2 cup red wine
6 gingersnap cookies, crumbled
1/4 teaspoon ground allspice
Sour cream, for serving (optional)

1. Place the chuck roast into the roasting pan.

2. Place remaining ingredients, except sour cream, in a large bowl. Stir to combine then pour over the roast.

3. Cover tightly with aluminum foil then cut 4 small slits into the foil for steaming purposes.

4. Place the pan on the rack in the lower position then close the door.

5. Set the Vent Release Valve to SEAL, lower the Sealing Lever to the SEAL position and set the timer.

6. Set the oven to 375°F and function to ROAST.

7. Cook for 3 hours then turn the Vent Release Valve to VENT and wait for all air to escape. Once vented, slowly raise the Sealing Lever and press the Door Release Button to open the door.

8. Remove pan, let meat rest for 10 minutes then slice, garnish as desired and serve with sour cream if desired.

Roasted Beet Salad

MAKES 4-6 SERVINGS

6 medium beets, scrubbed
Kosher salt and fresh pepper to taste
4 cups finely chopped kale or spinach
4 ounces goat or feta cheese, crumbled
1/2 cup toasted walnuts or pecans

The segments from 2 oranges
Zest and juice of 1 orange
2 tablespoons honey
3 tablespoons extra-virgin olive oil

1. Place beets on a square of aluminum foil then season with salt and pepper. Wrap the foil around the beets into a pouch then cut 4 small slits into the foil for steaming purposes and place in the roasting pan.

2. Place the pan on the rack in the lower position then close the door.

3. Set the Vent Release Valve to SEAL, lower the Sealing Lever to the SEAL position and set the timer.

4. Set the oven to 450°F and function to ROAST.

5. Cook for 50 minutes.

6. When cooking is complete, turn the Vent Release Valve to VENT and wait for all air to escape. Once vented, slowly raise the Sealing Lever and press the Door Release Button to open the door.

7. Remove foil packet and let stand until cool enough to handle. Using gloves, slip the skins off the beets and cut into slices then combine the beets, kale, cheese, nuts, salt, pepper and orange segments.

8. In a small bowl, whisk together the zest and juice from the orange, salt, pepper, honey and oil until blended then drizzle over the salad and serve.

Sausage Stuffed Peppers

MAKES 4 SERVINGS

1 pound bulk Italian sausage
2 cups leftover cooked white rice
1/2 cup jarred pasta sauce + 2 cups for the pan
1/2 small yellow onion, chopped
1 cup Parmesan cheese, shredded
Kosher salt and fresh pepper to taste
4 bell peppers, topped and seeded

1. In a large mixing bowl, combine the sausage, rice, 1/2 cup pasta sauce, onions, cheese, salt and pepper.

2. Divide sausage mixture between the bell peppers then place peppers into the roasting pan and pour remaining pasta sauce around them.

3. Place the pan on the rack in the lower position then close the door.

4. Set the Vent Release Valve to SEAL, lower the Sealing Lever to the SEAL position and set the timer.

5. Set the oven to 450°F and function to BAKE.

6. Cook for 45 minutes or until peppers are well browned and internal temperature of meat reaches 165°F on a meat thermometer.

7. When cooking is complete, turn the Vent Release Valve to VENT and wait for all air to escape. Once vented, slowly raise the Sealing Lever and press the Door Release Button to open the door.

8. Remove peppers, garnish as desired and serve with sauce.

Traditional chicken salad recipes typically call for boiled chicken. Using the leftover chicken or turkey that was roasted in the oven provides for better flavor than boiled chicken.

Roasted Chicken Salad

MAKES 6 SERVINGS

3 cups leftover chicken or turkey (from recipe on page 6, 80, 98 or 125)
1 celery stalk, chopped
1 small red onion, chopped
1/4 cup pecans, toasted
1 small apple, chopped
1/4 cup raisins
1/4 cup seedless grapes
2 tablespoons sweet relish
1/2 cup mayonnaise
1 tablespoon yellow mustard
1/2 teaspoon fresh lemon juice
Kosher salt and fresh pepper to taste

1. In a mixing bowl, toss together the chicken, celery, onions, pecans, apples, raisins and grapes.

2. In a separate mixing bowl, whisk together the relish, mayonnaise, mustard, lemon juice, salt and pepper.

3. Pour relish mixture over the chicken mixture and stir to combine well. Add mayonnaise if it seems too dry.

4. Garnish as desired and serve.

Teriyaki Chicken Wings

MAKES 4-5 SERVINGS

1 cup bottled teriyaki sauce
1 tablespoon soy sauce
2 tablespoons canola oil
2 teaspoons fresh ginger, chopped

2 garlic cloves, chopped
18 small chicken wings (about 3 pounds)
3 green onions, sliced
1 tablespoon sesame seeds

1. Preheat the oven to 450°F, set the function to BAKE and timer to 10 minutes.

2. In the roasting pan, toss together the teriyaki sauce, soy sauce, oil, ginger, garlic and wings.

3. Place the pan on the rack in the lower position then close the door.

4. Set the Vent Release Valve to SEAL, lower the Sealing Lever to the SEAL position and reset the timer.

5. Cook for 10 minutes then switch to BROIL for 10 minutes.

6. Cook until thickest part of chicken registers 165°F on a meat thermometer.

7. When cooking is complete, turn the Vent Release Valve to VENT and wait for all air to escape. Once vented, slowly raise the Sealing Lever and press the Door Release Button to open the door.

8. Remove wings, garnish as desired and serve with green onions and sesame seeds.

TIP

You can substitute the peanut butter for nut butter made from cashews or almonds if you are allergic to peanuts.

Thai Tilapia with Peanut Sauce

MAKES 4 SERVINGS

4 tilapia fillets
Kosher salt to taste
1/2 cup smooth peanut butter, microwaved until fluid
1/4 cup coconut milk
1 tablespoon soy sauce
2 tablespoons honey
2 garlic cloves, finely minced
1 tablespoon fresh ginger, finely minced
2 teaspoons dark sesame oil
Zest and juice from 1 lime

1. Preheat the oven to 450°F, set the function to BROIL and timer to 10 minutes.

2. Apply nonstick cooking spray to the drip/baking pan then place tilapia fillets on it. Season with salt.

3. In a bowl, whisk together remaining ingredients until smooth then spoon some peanut sauce over each fillet. Reserve the rest for serving.

4. Place the pan on the rack in the upper position then close the door.

5. Set the Vent Release Valve to SEAL, lower the Sealing Lever to the SEAL position and reset the timer.

6. Cook for 7-10 minutes or until just cooked through and fish flakes easily with a fork.

7. When cooking is complete, turn the Vent Release Valve to VENT and wait for all air to escape. Once vented, slowly raise the Sealing Lever and press the Door Release Button to open the door.

8. Remove tilapia, garnish as desired and serve with additional peanut sauce.

Unstuffed (Deconstructed) Cabbage Rolls

MAKES 4-6 SERVINGS

4 cups green cabbage, chopped

For the Sauce:
1 can (28 ounces) tomato puree
2 teaspoons dry mustard powder
2 tablespoons all purpose flour or cornstarch
2/3 cup granulated sugar or a substitute
1/3 cup apple cider vinegar
2 teaspoons kosher salt or to taste

For the Meat:
1 pound raw sage sausage or ground beef
1 small yellow onion, chopped
1 cup leftover cooked rice
8 gingersnap cookies
1/4 cup whole milk
1 large egg
1 tablespoon jarred beef bouillon base or to taste

1. Place the cabbage into the roasting pan.

2. In a bowl, whisk together all sauce ingredients. Set aside 1/2 cup of sauce then divide remaining sauce in half. Pour one half of sauce over the cabbage.

3. In a large bowl, combine all meat ingredients plus the 1/2 cup reserved sauce. Pour meat mixture over the cabbage then pat it down using your hands (wearing gloves if you prefer). Score it into 8 servings using a knife, cutting down to the cabbage layer. Pour over remaining sauce then score again to let the sauce flow under.

4. Cover tightly with aluminum foil then cut 4 small slits into the foil for steaming purposes.

5. Place the pan on the rack in the lower position then close the door.

6. Set the Vent Release Valve to SEAL, lower the Sealing Lever to the SEAL position and set the timer.

7. Set the oven to 450°F and function to BAKE.

8. Cook for 60 minutes.

9. When cooking is complete, turn the Vent Release Valve to VENT and wait for all air to escape. Once vented, slowly raise the Sealing Lever and press the Door Release Button to open the door.

10. Remove pan, garnish as desired and serve hot.

Oven Fried Chicken

MAKES 4-6 SERVINGS

1 cup all purpose flour
2 teaspoons kosher salt
1/2 teaspoon fresh pepper
1/2 teaspoon paprika
1/2 teaspoon dried sage
2 teaspoons onion powder
4-6 chicken pieces such as boneless, skinless breasts
3 tablespoons canola oil

1. Combine the flour, salt, pepper, paprika, sage and onion powder in a plastic zipper bag.

2. Add half of the chicken to the bag, shake well to coat then transfer to the roasting pan. Repeat with remaining chicken.

3. Drizzle oil evenly over chicken then place the pan on the rack in the lower position and close the door.

4. Set the Vent Release Valve to SEAL, lower the Sealing Lever to the SEAL position and set the timer.

5. Set the oven to 450°F and function to BAKE.

6. Cook for 35 minutes or until internal temperature of chicken registers 165°F on a meat thermometer.

7. When cooking is complete, turn the Vent Release Valve to VENT and wait for all air to escape. Once vented, slowly raise the Sealing Lever and press the Door Release Button to open the door.

8. Remove chicken, garnish as desired and serve.

Quinoa and Sweet Potato Bake

MAKES 4-6 SERVINGS

2 sweet potatoes, diced
1 small yellow onion, chopped
1 cup chopped kale or spinach
2 tablespoons fresh ginger, chopped
4 garlic cloves, chopped
1 cup fresh pineapple, chopped

3 tablespoons coconut oil or butter, melted
1 1/2 cups quinoa
2 cups vegetable stock
2 tablespoons apple cider vinegar
1 tablespoon curry powder
Kosher salt and fresh pepper to taste

1. Combine all ingredients in the roasting pan and stir.

2. Cover tightly with aluminum foil then cut 4 small slits into the foil for steaming purposes.

3. Place the pan on the rack in the lower position then close the door.

4. Set the Vent Release Valve to SEAL, lower the Sealing Lever to the SEAL position and set the timer.

5. Set the oven to 450°F and function to BAKE.

6. Cook for 45 minutes.

7. When cooking is complete, turn the Vent Release Valve to VENT and wait for all air to escape. Once vented, slowly raise the Sealing Lever and press the Door Release Button to open the door.

8. Remove, garnish as desired and serve.

Roast Garlic Chicken

MAKES 4 SERVINGS

1 whole chicken (4 pounds), legs tied
12 fresh garlic cloves
4 sprigs fresh rosemary
1 lemon, cut into wedges

2 sweet potatoes, chunked
1 large yellow onion, cut into wedges
1 tablespoon good quality olive oil
Kosher salt and fresh pepper to taste

1. Place the chicken into the roasting pan.

2. Place half of the garlic, rosemary and lemon pieces inside the chicken cavity then place other half as well as potatoes and onions around the chicken.

3. Drizzle all with the olive oil then season well with salt and pepper.

4. Place the pan on the rack in the lower position then close the door.

5. Set the Vent Release Valve to SEAL, lower the Sealing Lever to the SEAL position and set the timer.

6. Set the oven to 450°F and function to ROAST.

7. Cook for 35 minutes or until well browned and internal temperature of the chicken thigh registers 165°F on a meat thermometer.

8. When cooking is complete, turn the Vent Release Valve to VENT and wait for all air to escape. Once vented, slowly raise the Sealing Lever and press the Door Release Button to open the door.

9. Remove pan, let stand 10 minutes then carve, garnish as desired and serve.

Broiled Steak

MAKES 2 SERVINGS

2 New York strip steaks (1-inch thick, 10-12 ounces each)
2 teaspoons olive oil
Kosher salt and fresh pepper to taste
2 tablespoons unsalted butter, softened
1 garlic clove, minced
1/2 green onion, minced

1. Preheat the oven to 450°F, set the function to BROIL and timer to 10 minutes.

2. Rub each steak with oil, season liberally with salt and pepper then place on drip/baking pan.

3. Place the pan on the rack in the upper position then close the door.

4. Set the Vent Release Valve to SEAL, lower the Sealing Lever to the SEAL position and reset the timer.

5. Cook for 7 minutes then turn the Vent Release Valve to VENT and wait for all air to escape. Once vented, slowly raise the Sealing Lever and press the Door Release Button to open the door.

6. Remove pan, flip steaks over, place back in oven, repeat step 4 then cook for an additional 3-4 minutes or until desired doneness (about 10 minutes total cooking time for rare, 15 minutes for medium and 20 minutes for well-done).

7. While steaks are cooking, stir together the butter, garlic, green onions and a pinch of salt in a small bowl.

8. When steaks are done cooking, let rest for 5 minutes then top each with some of the butter mixture.

9. Adjust seasoning if needed, garnish as desired and serve hot.

Index

Wolfgang Puck

Pressure Oven Quick Start Guide

Before using this Quick Start Guide, please ensure that you have read the Instruction Manual fully and have become familiar with the import safeguards.

Warning: The oven exterior and door is hot during and after use. To prevent a burn injury we recommend always using protective hot pads or oven mitts when adding or removing items from the oven.

It is necessary to do a trial run of your oven to eliminate any protective substance on the heating elements. Conduct the trial run in a well-ventilated area as a small amount of smoke and odor may be detected. This is normal and should be expected. Follow the procedure in the manual for the trial run.

To cook in PRESSURE Mode:

1 Set the FUNCTION KNOB to the desired function and preheat the oven according to the recipe instructions.

2 Once preheated, press the DOOR RELEASE BUTTON to open door and add food.

3 Close the oven door and lower the SEALING LEVER to the SEAL position.

4 Turn the VENT RELEASE VALVE to the SEAL position.

5 Set the TIMER KNOB to the desired cooking time.

When cooking is complete in PRESSURE mode (see illustration below)

1 Set the TIMER KNOB to 0 (unless already off).

2 Turn the VENT RELEASE VALVE to the VENT position and wait until all steam has released.

3 Raise the SEALING LEVER to the STANDARD position.

4 Press the DOOR RELEASE BUTTON to open the door.

WARNING! Never attempt to raise the SEALING LEVER or open the door until all steam has been vented from the VENT RELEASE VALVE. Failure to do so could result in a scalding injury.

To cook in STANDARD Mode:

1 Set the FUNCTION KNOB to the desired function and preheat the oven according to the recipe instructions.

2 Once preheated press the DOOR RELEASE BUTTON to open door and add food.

3 Close the oven door and leave the SEALING LEVER to the STANDARD position.

4 Turn the VENT RELEASE VALVE to the VENT position.

5 Set the TIMER KNOB to the desired cooking time.

6 When cooking is complete, turn the TIMER to 0 (unless already off) and press the DOOR RELEASE BUTTON to open the door.

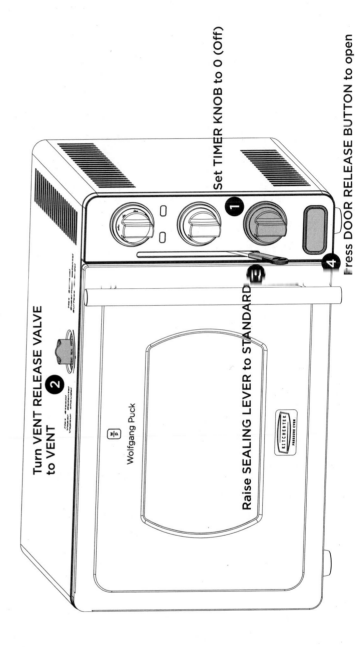

Turn VENT RELEASE VALVE to VENT ②

Wolfgang Puck

Raise SEALING LEVER to STANDARD

Set TIMER KNOB to 0 (Off)

Press DOOR RELEASE BUTTON to open

Wolfgang Puck

Pressure Oven Quick Start Guide

Type	Weight	Rack	PRESSURE MODE Temp (F)	PRESSURE MODE Time	STANDARD MODE Temp (F)	STANDARD MODE Time	US-FDA RECOMMENDED Internal Temp (F)
POULTRY							
Chicken (Whole)	3-4 lbs	Middle	450	35 min	350	2 hrs	165
Chicken (Whole)	5-6 lbs	Middle	450	40 min	350	2 to 2hrs 15min	165
Chicken (Whole)	7-8 lbs	Bottom	450	43 min	350	2 to 2 1/4 hrs	165
Chicken - 8pc Barbecue	3-4 lbs	Middle	450	20 min	350	1hr	165
Chicken - Butterflied	4 lbs	Middle	450	25 min	350	35 min	165
Chicken Breast, Boneless	< 1 lb	Middle	450	9 min	350	30-40 min	165
Chicken Breast, Boneless	1-2 lbs	Middle	450	10 min	350	40-45 min	165
Turkey, Unstuffed	9-10 lbs	Bottom	450	45 min	325	2hrs 45min to 3hrs	165
Turkey, Unstuffed	11-12 lbs	Bottom	450	49 min	325	3 hrs	165
Turkey, Unstuffed	13-14 lbs	Bottom	450	55 min	325	3hrs to 3hrs 45min	165
BEEF							
Ribeye Steak	10-12 oz	Upper	450	10 min	450	15 min	145
Braised Beef	4-5 lbs	Middle	375	2hrs 30min	325	3 hrs 30 min	145
Prime Rib	6.5 lbs	Bottom	450	90 min	400	2 hrs 30 min	145
Roast Beef (Eye Round)	6-7 lbs	Bottom	450	81 min	325	3 hrs 45 min	145
Roast Beef (Eye Round)	4-5 lbs	Bottom	450	78 min	325	2 hrs 30 min	145
PORK							
Pork Roast (Shoulder)	4-5 lbs	Middle	325	46 min	325	2 hrs 30 min	145[1]
Pork Roast (Shoulder)	6-7 lbs	Middle	325	49 min	325	3 hrs 30 min	145[1]
Fresh Ham (Shank)	10-11 lbs	Bottom	350	3 hrs	350	3.5-4 hrs	145[1]
Pork Loin	4-5 lbs	Middle	450	35 min	325	1 hr 15 min	145[1]
FISH							
Salmon Filet	< 1 lb	Middle	450	7 min	400	10-12 min	As Desired
Salmon Filet	1-2 bs	Middle	450	9 min	400	18-20 min	As Desired

[1] According to the US FDA cook pork, roasts, and chops to 145°F as measured with a food thermometer before removing meat from the heat source, with a three-minute rest time before carving or consuming. This will result in a product that is both safe and at its best quality - juicy and tender.
Visit www.foodsafety.gov for more tips.